GENERAL CONFERENCE ADDRESSES

———

GENERAL CONFERENCE ADDRESSES

JOURNAL EDITION
OCTOBER 2022

DESERET
BOOK

SALT LAKE CITY, UTAH

Book design © Deseret Book Company
Cover photo: LeManna/Getty Images
Interior photos: page 1: Valeri Vatel/Shutterstock; page 41: knape/Getty Images; page 80: Li Ding/Adobe Stock; page 108: Igor Stevanovic/Getty Images; page 147: bgfoto/Getty Images

October 2022 General Conference Addresses, Journal Edition by Deseret Book Company © by Intellectual Reserve, Inc.

DESERET BOOK is a registered trademark of Deseret Book Company.

Visit us at deseretbook.com

978-1-63993-083-8

Printed in the United States of America
North Star Printing, American Fork, UT

10   9   8   7   6   5   4   3   2   1

CONTENTS

SATURDAY EVENING SESSION

SUNDAY MORNING SESSION

CONTENTS

SUNDAY AFTERNOON SESSION

SATURDAY MORNING SESSION

OCTOBER 1, 2022

HELPING THE POOR AND DISTRESSED

PRESIDENT DALLIN H. OAKS
First Counselor in the First Presidency

Brothers and sisters, our beloved President Russell M. Nelson will address us later in this session. He has asked me to be the first speaker.

My subject today concerns what The Church of Jesus Christ of Latter-day Saints and its members give and do for the poor and distressed. I will also speak of similar giving by other good people. Giving to those in need is a principle in all Abrahamic religions and in others as well.

A few months ago, The Church of Jesus Christ of Latter-day Saints reported for the first time the extent of our humanitarian work worldwide.[1] Our 2021 expenditures for those in need in 188 countries worldwide totaled $906 million—almost a billion dollars. In addition, our members volunteered over 6 million hours of labor in the same cause.

Those figures are, of course, an incomplete report of our giving and helping. They do not include the personal services our members give individually as they minister to one another in called positions and voluntary member-to-member service. And our 2021 report makes no mention of what our members do individually through innumerable charitable organizations not formally connected with our Church. I begin with these.

In 1831, less than two years after the restored Church was organized, the Lord gave this revelation to guide its members and, I believe, all of His children worldwide:

"Behold, it is not meet that I should command in all things; for he that is compelled in all things, the same is a slothful and not a wise servant. . . .

"Verily I say, men should be anxiously engaged in a good cause, and do many things of their own free will, and bring to pass much righteousness;

"For the power is in them, wherein they are agents unto

themselves. And inasmuch as men do good they shall in nowise lose their reward."[2]

In more than 38 years as an Apostle and over 30 years of professional employment, I have seen many generous efforts by organizations and persons of the kind this revelation describes as "a good cause" and "bring[ing] to pass much righteousness." There are uncounted examples of such humanitarian service throughout the world, beyond our own borders and beyond our common knowledge. Contemplating this, I think of the Book of Mormon prophet-king Benjamin, whose sermon included this eternal truth: "When ye are in the service of your fellow beings ye are only in the service of your God."[3]

Much welfare and humanitarian service to our fellow beings is taught and practiced by The Church of Jesus Christ of Latter-day Saints and by us as its members. For example, we fast at the first of each month and contribute at least the equivalent of the uneaten meals to help those in need in our own congregations. The Church also makes enormous contributions for humanitarian and other services throughout the world.

Despite all that our Church does directly, most humanitarian service to the children of God worldwide is carried out by persons and organizations having no formal connection with our Church. As one of our Apostles observed: "God is using more than one people for the accomplishment of his great and marvelous work. . . . It is too vast, too arduous, for any one people."[4] As members of the restored Church, we need to be more aware and more appreciative of the service of others.

The Church of Jesus Christ is committed to *serving* those in need, and it is also committed to *cooperating* with others in that effort. We recently made a large gift to the United Nations World Food Programme. Over the many decades of our humanitarian work, two organizations stand out as key collaborators: projects with the Red Cross and Red Crescent agencies in dozens of countries have provided the children of God crucial relief during natural disasters and conflicts. Likewise, we have a long record of assistance with

Catholic Relief Services. These organizations have taught us much about world-class relief.

We have also had fruitful collaborations with other organizations, including Muslim Aid, Water for People, and IsraAID, to name just a few. While each humanitarian organization has its own areas of specialization, we share the common goal of relieving suffering among God's children. All of this is part of God's work for His children.

Modern revelation teaches that our Savior, Jesus Christ, is "the true light that lighteth every man that cometh into the world."[5] By this, all the children of God are enlightened to serve Him and one another to the best of their knowledge and ability.

The Book of Mormon teaches that "every thing which inviteth and enticeth to do good, and to love God, and to serve him, is inspired of God."[6]

Continuing:

"For behold, the Spirit of Christ is given to every man, that he may know good from evil; wherefore, I show unto you the way to judge; for every thing which inviteth to do good, and to persuade to believe in Christ, is sent forth by the power and gift of Christ. . . .

"And now, my brethren, . . . ye know the light by which ye may judge, which light is the light of Christ."[7]

Here are some examples of children of God helping other children of God with their vital needs for food, medical care, and teaching:

Ten years ago, the Kandharis, a Sikh husband and wife in the United Arab Emirates, personally launched a remarkable effort to feed the hungry. Through the Guru Nanak Darbar Sikh temple, they are currently serving over 30,000 vegetarian meals every weekend to anyone who enters their doors, regardless of religion or race. Dr. Kandhari explains, "We believe that all are one, we are children of one God, and we are here to serve humanity."[8]

The provision of medical and dental care to those in need is another example. In Chicago, I met a Syrian-American critical care physician, Dr. Zaher Sahloul. He is one of the founders of MedGlobal, which organizes medical professionals to volunteer their time, skills, knowledge, and leadership to help others in crises, such as in the Syrian war, where Dr. Sahloul risked his life in giving medical care to civilians. MedGlobal and similar organizations (including many Latter-day Saint professionals) demonstrate that God is moving professionals of faith to bring the poor needed relief worldwide.[9]

Many unselfish children of God are involved in teaching efforts, also worldwide. A good example, known to us through our humanitarian efforts, is the activity of a man known as Mr. Gabriel, who has been a refugee from various conflicts on several occasions. He recently observed that hundreds of thousands of refugee children in East Africa needed help to keep their hopes alive and their minds active. He organized other teachers in the refugee population into what they called "tree schools," where children were gathered for lessons under the shade of a tree. He did not wait for others to organize or direct but personally led efforts that have provided learning opportunities for thousands of primary school children during stressful years of displacement.

Of course, these three examples do not mean that everything said or done by organizations or individuals purporting to be good or of God is truly that. These examples do show that God inspires many organizations and individuals to do much good. It also shows that more of us should be recognizing the good done by others and supporting it as we have the time and means to do so.

Here are some examples of service the Church supports and which our members and other good people and organizations also support with individual donations of time and money:

I begin with religious freedom. In supporting that, we serve our own interests but also the interests of other religions. As our first President, Joseph Smith, taught, "We claim the privilege of worshiping Almighty God according to the dictates of our own conscience, and allow all men the same privilege, let them worship how, where, or what they may."[10]

Other examples of the restored Church's humanitarian and other assistance that are also supported voluntarily by our members are our well-known schools, colleges, and universities and our less-known but now published large donations for the relief of those suffering from the destructions and dislocations of natural disasters like tornadoes and earthquakes.

Other charitable activities our members support by their voluntary donations and efforts are too numerous to list, but just mentioning these few will suggest their variety and importance: combating racism and other prejudices; researching how to prevent and cure diseases; helping the disabled; supporting music organizations; and improving the moral and physical environment for all.

All of the humanitarian efforts of The Church of Jesus Christ of Latter-day Saints seek to follow the example of a righteous people described in the Book of Mormon: "And thus, in their prosperous circumstances, they did not send away any who were naked, or that were hungry, or that were athirst, or that were sick, . . . and they . . . were liberal to all, both old and young, both bond and free, both male and female, whether out of the church or in the church."[11]

I testify of Jesus Christ, whose light and Spirit guide all of the children of God in helping the poor and distressed throughout the world. In the name of Jesus Christ, amen.

Notes

1. See *Caring for Those in Need: 2021 Annual Report of The Church of Jesus Christ of Latter-day Saints* (2022).
2. Doctrine and Covenants 58:26–28.
3. Mosiah 2:17.
4. Orson F. Whitney, in Conference Report, Apr. 1928, 59.
5. Doctrine and Covenants 93:2; see also John 1:9.
6. Moroni 7:13.
7. Moroni 7:16, 18.
8. See "Sikhs and Latter-day Saints in UAE Join for Annual Service Project," Middle East Newsroom, Feb. 7, 2022, news-middleeast.ChurchofJesusChrist.org.
9. See "Who We Are," MedGlobal, medglobal.org.
10. Articles of Faith 1:11.
11. Alma 1:30.

JESUS CHRIST IS THE STRENGTH OF YOUTH

ELDER DIETER F. UCHTDORF

Of the Quorum of the Twelve Apostles

In preparing for this message today, I have felt strong promptings to address the young women and young men.

I am also speaking to those who used to be young, even to those who can't really remember it anymore.

And I speak to all who love our young people and want them to succeed in life.

For the rising generation, I have a message especially for you from our Savior, Jesus Christ.

The Savior's Message to You

My dear young friends, if the Savior were here right now, what would He say to you?

I believe He would start by expressing His deep love for you. He might say it with words, but it would also flow so strongly—just from His presence—that it would be unmistakable, reaching deep into your heart, filling your whole soul!

And yet, because we're all weak and imperfect, some concerns might creep into your mind. You might remember mistakes you've made, times you gave in to temptation, things you wish you hadn't done—or wish you had done better.

The Savior would sense that, and I believe He would assure you with words He has spoken in the scriptures:

"Fear not."[1]

"Doubt not."[2]

"Be of good cheer."[3]

"Let not your heart be troubled."[4]

I don't think He would make excuses for your mistakes. He wouldn't minimize them. No, He would ask you to repent—to leave your sins behind, to change, so He can forgive you. He would remind you that 2,000 years ago He took those sins upon Himself so

7

that you *could* repent. That is part of the plan of happiness gifted to us from our loving Heavenly Father.

Jesus might point out that your covenants with Him—made when you were baptized and renewed each time you partake of the sacrament—give you a special connection with Him. The kind of connection the scriptures describe as being yoked together so that, with His help, you can carry any burden.[5]

I believe the Savior Jesus Christ would want you to see, feel, and know that He is your strength. That with His help, there are no limits to what you can accomplish. That your potential is limitless. He would want you to see yourself the way He sees you. And that is very different from the way the world sees you.

The Savior would declare, in no uncertain terms, that you are a daughter or son of the Almighty God. Your Heavenly Father is the most glorious being in the universe, full of love, joy, purity, holiness, light, grace, and truth. And one day He wants you to inherit all He has.[6]

It is the reason why you're on the earth—to learn, grow, and progress and become everything your Father in Heaven has created you for.

To make this possible, He sent Jesus Christ to be your Savior. It's the purpose behind His great plan of happiness, His Church, His priesthood, the scriptures—all of it.

That is your destiny. *That* is your future. *That is your choice!*

Truth and Choices

At the heart of God's plan for your happiness is your power to choose.[7] Of course, your Heavenly Father wants you to choose eternal joy with Him, and He will help you to achieve it, but He would never force it upon you.

So He allows you to choose: Light or darkness? Good or evil? Joy or misery? Eternal life or spiritual death?[8]

It sounds like an easy choice, doesn't it? But somehow, here on earth, it seems more complicated than it ought to be.

The problem is that we don't always see things as clearly as we would like to. The Apostle Paul compared it to looking "through a glass, darkly."[9] There's a lot of confusion in the world about what is right and wrong. Truth gets twisted to make evil seem good and good seem evil.[10]

But when you earnestly seek the truth—eternal, unchanging truth—your choices become much clearer. Yes, you still have temptation and trials. Bad things still happen. Puzzling things. Tragic things. But you can manage when you know who you are, why you are here, and when you trust God.

So where do you find truth?

It is contained in the gospel of Jesus Christ. And the fulness of that gospel is taught in The Church of Jesus Christ of Latter-day Saints.

Jesus Christ said, "I am the way, the truth, and the life: no man cometh unto the Father, but by me."[11]

When you have important choices to make, Jesus Christ and His restored gospel are the best choice. When you have questions, Jesus Christ and His restored gospel are the best answer. When you feel weak, Jesus Christ is your strength.

He gives power to the weary; and to those who feel powerless, He increases strength.

They who wait upon the Lord will be renewed by His strength.[12]

For the Strength of Youth

To help you find the Way and to help you make Christ's doctrine the guiding influence in your life, The Church of Jesus Christ of Latter-day Saints has prepared a new resource, a revised version of *For the Strength of Youth*.

For over 50 years, *For the Strength of Youth* has been a guide for generations of Latter-day Saint youth. I always keep a copy in my pocket, and I share it with people who are curious about our standards. It has been updated and refreshed to better cope with the challenges and temptations of our day. The new version of *For the Strength of Youth* is available online in 50 different languages and will also be available in print. It will be a significant help for making choices in your life. Please embrace it as your own and share it with your friends.

This new version of *For the Strength of Youth* is subtitled *A Guide for Making Choices.*

To be very clear, the best guide you can possibly have for making choices is *Jesus Christ*. Jesus Christ *is* the strength of youth.

So the purpose of *For the Strength of Youth* is to point you to Him. It teaches you eternal truths of His restored gospel—truths about who you are, who He is, and what you can accomplish with His strength. It teaches you how to make righteous choices based on those eternal truths.[13]

It's also important to know what *For the Strength of Youth* does not do. It doesn't make decisions for you. It doesn't give you a "yes" or "no" about every choice you might ever face. *For the Strength of Youth* focuses on the foundation for your choices. It focuses on values, principles, and doctrine instead of every specific behavior.

The Lord, through His prophets, has always been guiding us in that direction. He is pleading with us to "increase [our] spiritual capacity to receive revelation."[14] He is inviting us to "hear Him."[15] He is calling us to follow Him in higher and holier ways.[16] And we are learning in a similar way every week in *Come, Follow Me.*

I suppose the guide could give you long lists of clothes you shouldn't wear, words you shouldn't say, and movies you shouldn't watch. But would that really be helpful in a global church? Would such an approach truly prepare you for a lifetime of Christlike living?

Joseph Smith said, "I teach them correct principles, and they govern themselves."[17]

And King Benjamin told his people in the Book of Mormon, "I cannot tell you all the things whereby ye may commit sin; for there are divers ways and means, even so many that I cannot number them."[18]

King Benjamin went on to say, "But this much I can tell you, . . . watch *yourselves*, and your thoughts, and your words, and your deeds, and observe the commandments of God, and continue in the faith of . . . our Lord, even unto the end of your lives."[19]

Is it wrong to have rules? Of course not. We all need them every day. But it is wrong to focus only on rules instead of focusing on the Savior. You need to know the whys and the hows and then consider the consequences of your choices. You need to put your trust in Jesus Christ. He will lead you the right way. He is your strength.[20]

The Power of True Doctrine

For the Strength of Youth is bold in declaring the doctrine of Jesus Christ. It is bold in inviting you to make choices based on Christ's doctrine. And it is bold in describing the blessings Jesus Christ promises those who follow His Way.[21]

President Russell M. Nelson taught: "When your greatest desire is to let God prevail [in your life], . . . many decisions become easier. . . . Many issues become nonissues! You know how best to groom yourself. You know what to watch and read, where to spend your time, and with whom to associate. You know what you want to accomplish. You know the kind of person you . . . want to become."[22]

A Higher Standard

Jesus Christ has very high standards for His followers. And the invitation to earnestly seek His will and live by His truths is the highest standard possible!

Important temporal and spiritual choices should not only be based on personal preference or what is convenient or popular.[23] The Lord is **not** saying, "Do whatever you want."

He is saying, "Let God prevail."

He is saying, "Come, follow me."[24]

He is saying, "Live in a holier, higher, more mature way."

He is saying, "Keep my commandments."

Jesus Christ is our perfect example, and we strive with all the energy of our soul to follow Him.

My dear friends, let me repeat, if the Savior were standing here today, He would express His endless love for you, His complete

11

confidence in you. He would tell you that you can do this. You can build a joyful, happy life because Jesus Christ is your strength. You can find confidence, peace, safety, happiness, and belonging now and eternally, because you will find all of it in Jesus Christ, in His gospel, and in His Church.

Of this I bear my solemn witness as an Apostle of the Lord Jesus Christ and leave you my heartfelt blessing in deep gratitude and love for you, in the name of Jesus Christ, amen.

Notes

1. Luke 5:10; 8:50; 12:7; Doctrine and Covenants 38:15; 50:41; 98:1.
2. Doctrine and Covenants 6:36.
3. Matthew 14:27; John 16:33; Doctrine and Covenants 61:36; 68:6; 78:18.
4. John 14:1, 27.
5. See Matthew 11:28–30.
6. See Doctrine and Covenants 84:38.
7. You might say the Father's plan was designed to allow you to express your desires through your choices so that you can receive the full results of what you desire. As Elder Dale G. Renlund taught, "Our Heavenly Father's goal in parenting is not to have His children *do* what is right; it is to have His children *choose* to do what is right and ultimately become like Him" ("Choose You This Day," *Ensign* or *Liahona*, Nov. 2018, 104).
8. See 2 Nephi 2:26–27.
9. 1 Corinthians 13:12.
10. See Isaiah 5:20.
11. John 14:6.
12. See Isaiah 40:29–31.
13. As Latter-day Saints, we are often known for what we do and don't do—our behaviors. This can be good, but it's even better to be known for what we *know* (the truths that drive our behaviors) and for *who* we know (the Savior—and how our love for Him inspires our behaviors).
14. Russell M. Nelson, "Revelation for the Church, Revelation for Our Lives," *Ensign* or *Liahona*, May 2018, 96.
15. See Russell M. Nelson, "Hear Him," *Ensign* or *Liahona*, May 2020, 88–92.
16. The principle-based approach of the new *For the Strength of Youth* guide is consistent with other recent initiatives introduced by the Savior's Church, including *Preach My Gospel*, ministering, the home-centered *Come, Follow Me* curriculum, the Children and Youth program, *Teaching in the Savior's Way*, and the new *General Handbook*. Clearly, the Lord is building our spiritual capacity. He is demonstrating increased trust in His covenant people in the latter days.
17. *Teachings of Presidents of the Church: Joseph Smith* (2007), 284.
18. Mosiah 4:29. In a way, this is what the Pharisees of Jesus's day tried to do. In their zeal to stop people from breaking the law, they compiled hundreds of rules based on their understanding of sacred writings. What the Pharisees got wrong was that they thought their rules would save them. Then, when the Savior appeared, they did not recognize Him.
19. Mosiah 4:30; emphasis added.
20. Another reason a principle-based approach is needed today is the increasing cultural diversity of the Lord's Church. Principles are eternal and universal. Specific rules or applications of those principles work well in some places but not in others. What unites us is Jesus Christ and the eternal truths He taught, even if specific applications vary over time and across cultures. So the problem with listing every possible do and don't isn't just that it's impractical and unsustainable. The problem is that it diverts our focus from the true Source of our strength, our Savior, Jesus Christ.
21. Many years ago, President Boyd K. Packer spoke these powerful words: "True doctrine,

understood, changes attitudes and behavior. The study of the doctrines of the gospel will improve behavior quicker than a study of behavior will improve behavior" ("Do Not Fear," *Ensign* or *Liahona*, May 2004, 79).

President Ezra Taft Benson taught a similar truth: "The Lord works from the inside out. The world works from the outside in. . . . The world would shape human behavior, but Christ can change human nature" ("Born of God," *Ensign*, Nov. 1985, 6).

When the Book of Mormon prophet Alma saw evil in the world around him, he turned to the word of God because he knew it "had more powerful effect upon the minds of the people than the sword, or anything else, which had happened unto them—therefore Alma thought it was expedient [to] try the virtue of the word of God" (Alma 31:5).

22. Russell M. Nelson, "Let God Prevail," *Ensign* or *Liahona*, Nov. 2020, 94. President Nelson exemplified this approach when he taught us about honoring the Sabbath day: "In my much younger years, I studied the work of others who had compiled lists of things to do and things *not* to do on the Sabbath. It wasn't until later that I learned from the scriptures that my conduct and my attitude on the Sabbath constituted a *sign* between me and my Heavenly Father. With that understanding, I no longer needed lists of dos and don'ts. When I had to make a decision whether or not an activity was appropriate for the Sabbath, I simply asked myself, 'What *sign* do I want to give to God?' That question made my choices about the Sabbath day crystal clear" ("The Sabbath Is a Delight," *Ensign* or *Liahona*, May 2015, 130).

23. Elder David A. Bednar taught that "principles of righteousness . . . help us to look beyond our personal preferences and self-centered desires by providing the precious perspective of eternal truth as we navigate the different circumstances, challenges, decisions, and experiences of mortality" ("The Principles of My Gospel," *Liahona*, May 2021, 123–24).

24. Luke 18:22.

SEEING MORE OF
JESUS CHRIST IN OUR LIVES

SISTER TRACY Y. BROWNING
Second Counselor in the Primary General Presidency

Brothers and sisters, how humbled I am to stand before you this morning. I knit my heart with yours in gratitude to be assembled, wherever you are across the world, to hear messages from prophets, apostles, seers, revelators, and leaders in God's kingdom. We figuratively become like the people of King Benjamin's day, pitching our tents and having our doors open and directed toward God's prophet on the earth,[1] President Russell M. Nelson.

I've had poor eyesight for as long as I can remember and have always needed the aid of prescription lenses to correct my vision. When I open my eyes every morning, the world appears very disorienting. Everything is out of focus, grainy, and distorted. Even my dear husband is more reminiscent of an abstract portrait than the well-loved and comforting figure he really is! My reflexive need, before I do anything else at the start of my day, is to reach for my glasses to help me make sense of my surroundings and enjoy a more vibrant experience as they help me navigate throughout my day.

Over the years, I've come to recognize that this behavior illustrates my daily dependence on two things: first, a tool that helps me to clarify, focus, and ground the world around me; and second, a need for tangible guidance to continually point me in the right direction. This simple, routine practice mirrors to me a significant observation about our relationship with our Savior, Jesus Christ.

In our lives that are often filled with questions, worries, pressures, and opportunities, our Savior's love for us individually and as His covenant children and also His teachings and laws are available daily resources that we can depend on to be a "light which shineth, . . . enlighten[ing our] eyes [and] quicken[ing our] understandings."[2] As we seek for the blessings of the Spirit in our lives, we will be able to, as Jacob taught, see "things as they really are, and . . . as they really will be."[3]

As covenant children of God, we have been uniquely blessed with a rich supply of divinely appointed tools to improve our spiritual vision. The words and teachings of Jesus Christ as recorded in scripture and messages from His chosen prophets and His Spirit received through daily prayer, regular temple attendance, and the weekly ordinance of the sacrament can help to restore peace and provide the necessary gift of discernment that brings Christ's light and His understanding to the corners of our life and in a world that may be cloudy. The Savior can also be our compass and our pilot as we steer through both the calm and the turbulent waters of life. He can make plain the correct path that leads us to our eternal destination. So what would He have us see, and where would He have us go?

Our dear prophet has taught that "our focus must be riveted on the Savior and His gospel" and that we must "strive to look unto Him in *every* thought."[4] President Nelson has also promised that "nothing invites the Spirit more than fixing your focus on Jesus Christ. . . . He will lead and guide *you* in your personal life if you will *make time for Him* in your life—each and every day."[5] Friends, Jesus Christ is both the purpose of our focus and the intent of our destination. To help us to remain fixed and heading in the right direction, the Savior invites us to see our lives *through Him* in order to see *more of Him* in our lives. I've come to learn more about this specific invitation through my study of the Old Testament.

The law of Moses was given to the early Israelites as a preparatory gospel, designed to ready the people for a higher covenant relationship with God through Jesus Christ.[6] The law, rich with symbolism pointing believers to "look forward to the coming" and Atonement of Jesus Christ,[7] was meant to help the people of Israel focus on the Savior by practicing faith in Him, His sacrifice, and His laws and commandments in their lives[8]—it was intended to bring them to a greater understanding of their Redeemer.

Just as we are today, God's ancient people were invited to see their lives *through Him* in order to see *more of Him* in their lives. But by the time of the Savior's ministry, the Israelites had lost sight of Christ in their observances, setting Him aside and adding to the law unauthorized practices that had no instructive symbolism pointing to the true and only source of their salvation and redemption—Jesus Christ.[9]

The everyday world of the Israelites had become disoriented and obscure. The children of Israel, in this state, believed that the practices and rituals of the law were the path to personal salvation and in part reduced the law of Moses to a set of protocols administered to rule civilian life.[10] This required the Savior to restore focus and clarity to His gospel.

Ultimately a great portion of the Israelites rejected His message, even going so far as to accuse the Savior—He who *gave* the law and declared that He *was* "the law, and the light"[11]—of breaking it. Yet Jesus in His Sermon on the Mount, speaking on the law of Moses, declared, "Think not that I am come to destroy the law, or the prophets: I am not come to destroy, but to fulfil."[12] Then the Savior, through His eternal Atonement, ended the codes, regulations, and ceremonial practices observed by the people of Israel at that time. His final sacrifice led the shift from sacrificial burnt offerings to our rendering of "a broken heart and a contrite spirit,"[13] from the ordinance of sacrifice to the ordinance of sacrament.

President M. Russell Ballard, teaching on the subject, said, "In a sense, the sacrifice changed from the *offering* to the *offerer*."[14] When we bring our offering to the Savior, we are being invited to see more of Jesus Christ in our lives, as we humbly submit our will to Him in recognition and understanding of His perfect submission to the will of the Father. When we fix our sight on Jesus Christ, we recognize and we understand that He is the only source and way to receive forgiveness and redemption, even unto eternal life and exaltation.

As an early follower of the gospel, I encountered many who observed and perceived changes in my behaviors, practices, and choices after I joined the Church. They were curious about the "whys" of what they were seeing—why I chose to be baptized and join *this* congregation of believers, even The Church of Jesus Christ of Latter-day Saints; why I refrain from certain practices on the Sabbath; why I'm faithful in keeping the Word of Wisdom; why I read the Book of

Mormon; why I believe in and incorporate the teachings of modern-day prophets and apostles into my life; why I attend weekly Church meetings; why I invite others to "*come and see, come and help, . . . come and stay,*"[15] and "*come and belong.*"[16]

At the time, those questions felt overwhelming and, transparently, sometimes accusatory. But as I grappled with people's scrutiny, I came to realize that their probing was, in fact, my first invitation to pick up and put on a pair of spiritual lenses to clarify, focus, and solidify what motivated my adherence to gospel practices and standards. What was the source of my testimony? Was I only carrying out "outward performances" without allowing those practices connected to God's laws to "strengthen [my] faith in Christ"[17] or to demonstrate understanding that *Jesus Christ is the only source of power in my observances*?

Through rigorous effort to look *to and for* Jesus Christ in my every thought and deed, my eyes were enlightened and my understanding quickened to recognize that Jesus Christ was calling for me to "come unto" Him.[18] From this early season of discipleship in my youth, I can recall an invitation extended to me by the missionaries to join them as they taught the gospel to a group of young girls about my age. One evening, as we were seated in the family home of one of these young women, their tender question of why I believe pricked my heart and allowed me to testify to them with deepened understanding of the Lord's vision about the spiritual motivations of my discipleship and has refined my testimony going forward.

I learned then, as I know now, that our Savior, Jesus Christ, directs our feet to meetinghouses each week to partake of His sacrament, to the house of the Lord to make covenants with Him, to the scriptures and teachings of prophets to learn of His words. He directs our mouths to testify of Him, our hands to lift and serve as He would lift and serve, our eyes to see the world and each other as He does—"as they really are, and . . . as they really will be."[19] And as we allow Him to direct us in all things, we receive testimony that "all things denote there is a God,"[20] because where we look for Him we will find Him[21]—each and every day. This I testify in the sacred name of Jesus Christ, amen.

Notes

1. See Mosiah 2:5–6.
2. Doctrine and Covenants 88:11.
3. Jacob 4:13.
4. Russell M. Nelson, "Drawing the Power of Jesus Christ into Our Lives," *Ensign* or *Liahona*, May 2017, 41.
5. Russell M. Nelson, "Make Time for the Lord," *Liahona*, Nov. 2021, 120, 121.
6. See Gib Kocherhans, "Reflections on the Law of Moses: Old Testament Apostasy in Context," *Ensign*, June 1981, 14–21.
7. Alma 25:15.
8. See Alma 25:16.
9. See Kocherhans, "Reflections on the Law of Moses," 14–21.
10. See Stephen E. Robinson, "The Law after Christ," *Ensign*, Sept. 1983, 69–73.
11. 3 Nephi 15:9.
12. Matthew 5:17.
13. 2 Nephi 2:7.
14. M. Russell Ballard, "The Law of Sacrifice," *Ensign*, Oct. 1998, 10; *Liahona*, Mar. 2002, 16.
15. Dieter F. Uchtdorf, "Missionary Work: Sharing What Is in Your Heart," *Ensign* or *Liahona*, May 2019, 17.
16. Dieter F. Uchtdorf, "Come and Belong," *Ensign* or *Liahona*, May 2020, 106.
17. Alma 25:15–16.
18. Matthew 11:28.
19. Jacob 4:13.
20. Alma 30:44.
21. See Jeremiah 29:13.

A FRAMEWORK FOR PERSONAL REVELATION

ELDER DALE G. RENLUND
Of the Quorum of the Twelve Apostles

Like many of you, I have been greatly influenced by Elder Dieter F. Uchtdorf over the years. That explains, at least in part, what I am about to say.[1] So, with apologies to him . . .

Well-trained airplane pilots fly within the capacity of their aircraft and follow directions from air traffic controllers regarding runway use and flight path. Simply stated, pilots operate within a framework. No matter how brilliant or talented they are, only by flying within this framework can pilots safely unleash the enormous potential of an airplane to accomplish its miraculous objectives.

In a similar way, we receive personal revelation within a framework. After baptism, we are given a majestic yet practical gift, the gift of the Holy Ghost.[2] As we strive to stay on the covenant path,[3] it is "the Holy Ghost . . . [that] will show [us] all things [that we] should do."[4] When we are unsure or uneasy, we can ask God for help.[5] The Savior's promise could not be clearer: "Ask, and it shall be given you; . . . for every one that asketh receiveth."[6] With the help of the Holy Ghost, we can transform our divine nature into our eternal destiny.[7]

The promise of personal revelation through the Holy Ghost is awe-inspiring, much like an airplane in flight. And like airplane pilots, we need to understand the framework within which the Holy Ghost functions to provide personal revelation. When we operate within the framework, the Holy Ghost can unleash astonishing insight, direction, and comfort. Outside of that framework, no matter our brilliance or talent, we can be deceived and crash and burn.

The scriptures form the first element of this framework for personal revelation.[8] Feasting on the words of Christ, as found in the scriptures, stimulates personal revelation. Elder Robert D. Hales said: "When we want to speak to God, we pray. And when we want Him to speak to us, we search the scriptures."[9]

The scriptures also teach us how to receive personal revelation.[10] And we ask for what is right and good[11] and not for what is contrary to God's will.[12] We do not "ask amiss," with improper motives to promote our own agenda or to fulfill our own pleasure.[13] Above all, we are to ask Heavenly Father in the name of Jesus Christ,[14] believing that we will receive.[15]

A second element of the framework is that we receive personal revelation only within our purview and not within the prerogative of others. In other words, we take off and land in our appointed runway. The importance of well-defined runways was learned early in the history of the Restoration. Hiram Page, one of the Eight Witnesses to the Book of Mormon, claimed to be receiving revelations for the entire Church. Several members were deceived and wrongly influenced.

In response, the Lord revealed that "no one shall be appointed to receive commandments and revelations in this church excepting my servant Joseph Smith . . . until I shall appoint . . . another in his stead."[16] Doctrine, commandments, and revelations for the Church are the prerogative of the living prophet, who receives them from the Lord Jesus Christ.[17] That is the prophet's runway.

Years ago, I received a phone call from an individual who had been arrested for trespassing. He told me it had been revealed to him that additional scripture was buried under the ground floor of a building he tried to enter. He claimed that once he obtained the additional scripture, he knew he would receive the gift of translation, bring forth new scripture, and shape the doctrine and direction of the Church. I told him that he was mistaken, and he implored me to pray about it. I told him I would not. He became verbally abusive and ended the phone call.[18]

I did not need to pray about this request for one simple but profound reason: only the prophet receives revelation *for the Church*. It would be "contrary to the economy of God"[19] for others to receive such revelation, which belongs on the prophet's runway.

Personal revelation rightly belongs to individuals. You can receive revelation, for example, about where to live, what career path to follow, or whom to marry.[20] Church leaders may teach doctrine and share inspired counsel, but the responsibility for these decisions rests with you. That is your revelation to receive; that is your runway.

A third element of the framework is that personal revelation will be in harmony with the commandments of God and the covenants we have made with Him. Consider a prayer that goes something like this: "Heavenly Father, Church services are boring. May I worship Thee on the Sabbath in the mountains or on the beach? May I be excused from going to church and partaking of the sacrament but still have the promised blessings of keeping the Sabbath day holy?"[21] In response to such a prayer, we can anticipate God's response: "My child, I have already revealed my will regarding the Sabbath day."

When we ask for revelation about something for which God has already given clear direction, we open ourselves up to misinterpreting our feelings and hearing what we want to hear. A man once told me about his struggles to stabilize his family's financial situation. He had the idea to embezzle funds as a solution, prayed about it, and felt he had received affirmative revelation to do so. I knew he had been deceived because he sought revelation contrary to a commandment of God. The Prophet Joseph Smith warned, "Nothing is a greater injury to the children of men than to be under the influence of a false spirit, when they think they have the Spirit of God."[22]

Some might point out that Nephi violated a commandment when he slew Laban. However, this exception does not negate the rule—the rule that personal revelation will be in harmony with God's commandments. No simple explanation of this episode is completely satisfactory, but let me highlight some aspects. The episode did not begin with Nephi asking if he could slay Laban. It was not something he wanted to do. Killing Laban was not for Nephi's personal benefit but to provide scriptures to a future nation and a covenant people. And Nephi was sure that it was revelation in fact, in this case, it was a commandment from God.[23]

The fourth element of the framework is to recognize what God has already revealed to you personally, while being open to further revelation from Him. If God has answered a question and the circumstances have not changed, why would we expect the answer to be different? Joseph Smith stumbled into this problematic scenario in 1828. The first portion of the Book of Mormon had been translated, when Martin Harris, a benefactor and early scribe, asked Joseph for permission to take the translated pages and show them to his wife. Unsure of what to do, Joseph prayed for guidance. The Lord told him not to let Martin take the pages.

Martin requested that Joseph ask God again. Joseph did so, and the answer was, not surprisingly, the same. But Martin begged Joseph to ask a third time, and Joseph did so. This time God did not say no. Instead, it was as though God said, "Joseph, you know how I feel about this, but you have your agency to choose." Feeling himself relieved of the constraint, Joseph decided to allow Martin to take 116 manuscript pages and show them to a few family members. The translated pages were lost and never recovered. The Lord severely rebuked Joseph.[24]

Joseph learned, as the Book of Mormon prophet Jacob taught: "Seek not to counsel the Lord, but to take counsel from his hand. For . . . he counseleth in wisdom."[25] Jacob cautioned that unfortunate things happen when we ask for things we should not. He foretold that the people in Jerusalem would seek "for things that they could not understand," look "beyond the mark," and completely overlook the Savior of the world.[26] They stumbled because they asked for things they would not and could not understand.

If we have received personal revelation for our situation and the circumstances have not changed, God has already answered our question.[27] For example, we sometimes ask repeatedly for reassurance that we have been forgiven. If we have repented, been filled with joy and peace of conscience, and received a remission of our sins, we do not need to ask again but can trust the answer God has already given.[28]

Even as we trust God's prior answers, we need to be open to further personal revelation. After all, few of life's destinations are reached via a nonstop flight. We should recognize that personal revelation may be received "line upon line" and "precept upon precept,"[29] that revealed direction can be and frequently is incremental.[30]

The elements of the framework for personal revelation are overlapping and mutually reinforcing. But within that framework, the Holy Ghost can and will reveal everything we need to soar onto and maintain momentum on the covenant path. Thus we can be blessed by the power of Jesus Christ to become what Heavenly Father wants us to be. I invite you to have the confidence to claim personal revelation for yourself, understanding what God has revealed, consistent with the scriptures and the commandments He has given through His appointed prophets and within your own purview and agency. I know that the Holy Ghost can and will show you all things that you should do.[31] In the name of Jesus Christ, amen.

Notes

1. Elder Dieter F. Uchtdorf has consistently and effectively used analogies related to aircraft to teach important gospel principles. For example, he recently linked pilots' preflight checklists to teaching like the Savior in "A Teacher's Checklist" ([broadcast for teachers, June 12, 2022], broadcasts.ChurchofJesusChrist.org).
2. The Holy Ghost is the third member of the Godhead, is often referred to as the Spirit or the Spirit of God, and performs vital roles in the plan of salvation. He bears witness of the Father and the Son, reveals the truth of all things, sanctifies those who have repented and been baptized, and is the Holy Spirit of Promise (see Guide to the Scriptures, "Holy Ghost," scriptures .ChurchofJesusChrist.org).
3. See 2 Nephi 31:19–21; Mosiah 4:8. There is no other way whereby we "can be saved in the kingdom of God." Wishing otherwise will not create an alternative path.
4. 2 Nephi 32:5; see also Doctrine and Covenants 84:43–44.
5. See 2 Nephi 32:4; Russell M. Nelson, "Revelation for the Church, Revelation for Our Lives," *Ensign* or *Liahona*, May 2018, 93–96.
6. Matthew 7:7–8.
7. See "The Family: A Proclamation to the World"; "Young Women Theme"; *General Handbook: Serving in The Church of Jesus Christ of Latter-day Saints*, 27.0; 27.2, ChurchofJesusChrist.org.
8. See 2 Nephi 32:3.
9. Robert D. Hales, "Holy Scriptures: The Power of God unto Our Salvation," *Ensign* or *Liahona*, Nov. 2006, 26–27.
10. The scriptures teach that the voice of the Holy Ghost is mild and still, like a whisper—not loud or noisy; it is simple, quiet, and plain; it can be piercing and burning; it affects both mind and heart; it brings peace, joy, and hope—not fear, anxiety, and worry; it invites us to do good—not evil; and it is enlightening and delicious—not mystifying. See 1 Kings 19:11–12; Omni 1:25; Alma 32:28; Helaman 5:30–33; 3 Nephi 11:3; Moroni 7:16–17; Doctrine and Covenants 6:22–24; 8:2–3; 9:8–9; 11:12–14; 85:6; Boyd K. Packer, "The Candle of the Lord," *Ensign*, Jan. 1983, 51–56; Russell M. Nelson, "Hear Him," *Ensign* or *Liahona*, May 2020, 88–92; Russell M. Nelson, "Embrace the Future with Faith," *Ensign* or *Liahona*, Nov. 2020, 73–76; Russell M. Nelson, "Revelation for the Church, Revelation for Our Lives," 93–96.
11. See 3 Nephi 18:20; Moroni 7:26; Doctrine and Covenants 88:64–65.
12. See Helaman 10:5; Doctrine and Covenants 46:30.
13. James 4:3; see James 4:3, New International Version; 2 Nephi 4:35; Doctrine and Covenants 8:10; 46:7; 88:64–65.

14. See Doctrine and Covenants 88:64–65; Guide to the Scriptures, "Prayer," scriptures.Churchof JesusChrist.org.

15. See 3 Nephi 18:20; Moroni 7:26.

16. Doctrine and Covenants 28:2, 7.

17. See Doctrine and Covenants 21:4–5.

18. Fortunately, arrangements were made for him to receive the help and treatment he really needed.

19. *Teachings of Presidents of the Church: Joseph Smith* (2007), 197.

20. See Thomas S. Monson, "Whom Shall I Marry?," *New Era*, Oct. 2004, 4.

21. See Doctrine and Covenants 59:9–16.

22. Joseph Smith, in *Times and Seasons*, Apr. 1, 1842, 744, josephsmithpapers.org.

23. The Lord often does change, amend, or make exceptions to His revealed commandments, but these are made through *prophetic* revelation and not *personal* revelation. *Prophetic* revelation comes through God's duly appointed prophet according to God's wisdom and understanding. These exceptions include the Lord's revelation to Moses and Joshua to kill the inhabitants of the land of Canaan despite His commandment "Thou shalt not kill" (Exodus 20:13). The Lord, through His prophet, can and will revise *His* commandments for *His* purposes. We are not free, however, through *personal* revelation to alter or ignore established commandments that God has revealed to His Church through the prophet.

    See 1 Nephi 4:12–18; for a fuller discussion, see Joseph Spencer, *1st Nephi: A Brief Theological Introduction* (2020), 66–80.

24. For the full account of the 116 manuscript pages, see *Saints: The Story of the Church of Jesus Christ in the Latter Days*, vol. 1, *The Standard of Truth, 1815–1846* (2018), 44–53; see also Doctrine and Covenants 3:5–15; 10:1–5.

25. Jacob 4:10.

26. See Jacob 4:14–16.

27. Joseph Smith taught, "We never enquire at the hand of God for special revelation only in the case of their being no previous revelation to suit the case" (in History, 1838–1856 [Manuscript History of the Church], volume A-1, 286–87, josephsmithpapers.org).

28. See Mosiah 4:3. When we continue to feel guilt and regret after sincere and intentional repentance, it is usually because of a lack of faith in Jesus Christ and in His ability to completely forgive and heal us. Sometimes we believe forgiveness is for others but does not completely apply to us. That is simply a lack of faith in what the Savior can accomplish because of His infinite Atonement.

29. See Isaiah 28:10; 2 Nephi 28:30; David A. Bednar, "Line upon Line, Precept upon Precept," *New Era*, Sept. 2010, 3–7.

30. But if God has not given you revelation, keep asking. As Elder Richard G. Scott taught: "Proceed with trust. . . . When you are living righteously and are acting with trust, God will not let you proceed too far without a warning impression if you have made the wrong decision" ("Using the Supernal Gift of Prayer," *Ensign* or *Liahona*, May 2007, 10).

31. See 2 Nephi 32:5.

LET DOING GOOD BE OUR NORMAL

ELDER RAFAEL E. PINO
Of the Seventy

I will always be grateful for my assignments in the Church that have taken me to live in different countries. We found in each one of these countries a great diversity and extraordinary people with different customs and traditions.

We all have customs and traditions that are personal, from our family, or from the community in which we live, and we hope to keep all those that align with the principles of the gospel. Edifying customs and traditions are fundamental to our efforts to stay on the covenant path, and those that are an obstacle, we ought to reject.

A custom is the practice or the frequent and habitual way of thinking for a person, culture, or tradition. Frequently, the things we think and do in a habitual way we recognize as normal.

Allow me to illustrate this: Patricia, my beloved wife, loves to drink coconut water and then to eat the coconut. During our first visit to Puebla, Mexico, we went to a place where we bought a coconut. After drinking the water, my wife asked them to cut the coconut and bring her the flesh to eat. When it came, it was reddish. They had sprinkled it with chili! Sweet coconut with chili! That seemed so strange to us. But later we learned that the strange ones were my wife and I, who did not eat coconut with chili. In Mexico, however, it is not rare; it is very normal.

On another occasion we were eating in Brazil with some friends, and they served us avocado. Just as we were about to sprinkle salt on it, our friends said to us, "What are you doing? We already put sugar on the avocado!" Avocado with sugar! That seemed so odd to us. But then we learned that the odd ones were my wife and I, who did not eat avocado with sugar. In Brazil, avocado sprinkled with sugar is normal.

What is normal for some may be odd for others, depending on their customs and traditions.

Which customs and traditions are normal in our lives?

President Russell M. Nelson has said: "Today we often hear about 'a new normal.' If you really want to embrace a new normal, I invite you to turn your heart, mind, and soul increasingly to our Heavenly Father and His Son, Jesus Christ. Let that be *your* new normal" ("A New Normal," *Ensign* or *Liahona*, Nov. 2020, 118).

This invitation is for all. It does not matter whether we are poor or rich, educated or uneducated, old or young, sick or healthy. He invites us to let the normal things in our lives be those which help keep us on the covenant path.

No country contains the totality of what is good or admirable. Therefore, as Paul and the Prophet Joseph Smith taught:

"If there is anything virtuous, lovely, or of good report or praiseworthy, we seek after these things" (Articles of Faith 1:13).

"If there be any praise, think on these things" (Philippians 4:8).

Note that this is an exhortation, not merely a commentary.

I would like all of us to take a moment to meditate on our customs and the way they are influencing our families.

Among the marvelous habits that should be normal for members of the Church are these four:

1. Personal and family study of the scriptures. To become converted to the Lord Jesus Christ, each person is responsible for learning the gospel. Parents are responsible for teaching the gospel to their children (see Doctrine and Covenants 68:25; 93:40).

2. Personal and family prayer. The Savior commands us to pray always (see Doctrine and Covenants 19:38). Prayer allows us to communicate personally with our Heavenly Father in the name of His Son, Jesus Christ.

3. Weekly sacrament meeting attendance (see 3 Nephi 18:1–12; Moroni 6:5–6). We do so to remember Jesus Christ as we take the sacrament. In this ordinance the members of the Church renew their covenant of taking upon themselves the name of the Savior, of always remembering

Him, and of keeping His commandments (see Doctrine and Covenants 20:77, 79).

4. Frequent participation in temple and family history work. This work is the means of uniting and sealing families for eternity (see Doctrine and Covenants 128:15).

How do we feel when we hear these four things? Are they part of our normal lives?

There are many other traditions that could be part of the normality we have adopted, thus letting God prevail in our lives.

How can we determine what will be the normal things in our life and in our family? In the scriptures we find a great model; in Mosiah 5:15 it says, "I would that ye should be steadfast and immovable, always abounding in good works."

I love these words because we know that the things that become normal in our lives are those that we repeat again and again. If we are steadfast and immovable in doing good, our customs will be in accordance with the principles of the gospel and they will help us to stay on the covenant path.

President Nelson has also counseled: "Embrace your new normal by repenting daily. Seek to be increasingly pure in thought, word, and deed. Minister to others. Keep an eternal perspective. Magnify your callings. And whatever your challenges, my dear brothers and sisters, live each day so that *you* are more prepared to meet your Maker" ("A New Normal," 118).

Now it is not odd for either my wife, Patricia, or for me to eat coconut with chili and avocado with sugar—in fact, we like it. However, exaltation is something much more transcendent than a sense of taste; it is a topic related to eternity.

I pray that our normality may allow us to experience that state of "never-ending happiness" (Mosiah 2:41) that is promised to those who keep the commandments of God and that, while doing so, we may be able to say, "And it came to pass that we lived after the manner of happiness" (2 Nephi 5:27).

My brothers and sisters, I testify of the 15 men whom we sustain as prophets, seers, and revelators, including our beloved prophet, President Russell M. Nelson. I testify that The Church of Jesus Christ of Latter-day Saints is true. I especially testify of Jesus Christ, our Savior and Redeemer, in the name of Jesus Christ, amen.

THE ETERNAL PRINCIPLE OF LOVE

ELDER HUGO MONTOYA
Of the Seventy

The eternal principle of love is manifested by living the two great commandments: love God with all your heart, soul, mind, and strength and love your neighbor as yourself.[1]

I remember my first winter living here in Utah—snow everywhere. Coming from the Sonoran Desert, the first days I was enjoying it, but after a few days I realized that I had to get up earlier to remove the snow from the driveway.

One morning, in the middle of a snowstorm, I was sweating, shoveling snow, and I saw my neighbor opening his garage across the street. He's older than I am, so I thought if I finished soon, I could help him. So raising my voice, I asked him, "Brother, do you need help?"

He smiled and said, "Thank you, Elder Montoya." Then he pulled a snowblower out of his garage, started the engine, and in a few minutes he removed all the snow in front of his house. He then crossed the street with his machine and asked me, "Elder, do you need help?"

With a smile I said, "Yes, thank you."

We are willing to help each other because we love each other, and my brother's needs become my needs, and mine become his. No matter what language my brother speaks or what country he comes from, we love each other because we are brothers, children of the same Father.

When ministering was announced, President Russell M. Nelson said, "We will implement a newer, holier approach to caring for and ministering to others."[2] To me, *holier* means more personal, deeper, more like the Savior's way: "Have love one to another,"[3] one by one.

It is not enough to avoid being a stumbling block for others; it is not enough to notice the needy on the road and pass by. Let us take advantage of every opportunity to help our neighbor, even if it is the first and only time we meet him or her in this life.

Why is love for God the first great commandment?

I think it's because of what He means to us. We are His children, He oversees our welfare, we are dependent on Him, and His love protects us. His plan includes agency; therefore, we will likely make some mistakes.

He also allows us to be tested and tempted. But whether we are making some mistakes or falling into temptation, the plan provides a Savior so we can be redeemed and return to the presence of God.

Adversity in our lives can cause doubt about the fulfillment of the promises that have been made to us. Please trust in our Father. He always keeps His promises, and we can learn what He wants to teach us.

Even when we do what is right, the circumstances in our life can change from good to bad, from happiness to sadness. God answers our prayers according to His infinite mercy and love and in His own time.

- The brook where Elijah drank water dried up.[4]
- Nephi's fine steel bow was broken.[5]
- A young boy was discriminated against and expelled from school.
- A long-awaited-for child died within days of being born.

Circumstances change.

When circumstances change from good and positive to bad and negative, we can still be happy because happiness does not depend on the circumstances but on our attitude toward the circumstances. President Nelson said, "The joy we feel has little to do with the circumstances of our lives and everything to do with the focus of our lives."[6]

We can sit back and wait for circumstances to change on their own, or we can look for and bring about new circumstances.

- Elijah walked to Zarephath, where a widow gave him food and drink.[7]
- Nephi made a wooden bow and hunted animals to eat.[8]
- The young boy sat listening and taking notes by the window, and today he is an elementary school teacher.
- The couple have developed a great faith in the Savior Jesus

Christ and trust in the plan of salvation. Their love for the long-awaited child who died suddenly is greater than their grief.

When I hear the questions "Heavenly Father, are you really there? And do you hear and answer [every] child's prayer?,"[9] I like to answer: "He has been, He is, and He will always be there for you and me. I am His son, He is my Father, and I am learning to be a good father, as He is."

My wife and I always try to be there for our children at any time, under any condition, and by any means. Each child is unique; their worth to God is great, and no matter what challenges, sins, and weaknesses they have, God loves them, and so do we.

When I received this call as a General Authority, on the last day before our travel to Salt Lake, all my children and their families were together in our home for a family home evening, where we expressed our love and gratitude. After the lesson, I gave a priesthood blessing to each one of my children. Everyone was in tears. After the blessings, my oldest son expressed words of gratitude on behalf of everyone for the great love that we had given them from the day they were born until then.

Bless your children, whether they are 5 or 50 years old. Be with them; be for them. Although providing is a responsibility established by divine design, we must not forget to share joyful time with our children.

Our Heavenly Father's love for each of His children is real. He is there for each one. I don't know how He does it, but He does. He and His Firstborn are one in doing the work and glory of the Father "to bring to pass the immortality and eternal life of man."[10] They have sent us the Holy Ghost to guide us, to warn us, and to comfort us if necessary.

He instructed His Beloved Son to create this beautiful earth. He instructed Adam and Eve and gave unto them their agency. He has been sending messengers for years and years so that we can receive His love and His commandments.

He was in the Sacred Grove answering young Joseph's sincere question and calling him by his name. He said: "This is My Beloved Son. Hear Him!"[11]

I believe that the supreme demonstration of God's love for us happened in Gethsemane, where the Son of the living God prayed, "O my Father, if it be possible, let this cup pass from me: nevertheless not as I will, but as thou wilt."[12]

I have noticed that the small portion that I can understand of the Atonement of Jesus Christ increases my love for the Father and His Son, decreases my desire to sin and to be disobedient, and increases my willingness to be better and do better.

Jesus walked with no fear and with no doubt to Gethsemane, trusting in His Father, knowing that He must tread the winepress alone. He endured all pain and all humiliation. He was accused, judged, and crucified. During His own agony and suffering on the cross, Jesus focused on the needs of His mother and His beloved disciple. He offered His life.

On the third day He was resurrected. The tomb is empty; He stands at the right hand of His Father. They hope we will choose to keep our covenants and return to Their presence. This second estate is not our final estate; we do not belong to this earthly home, but rather we are eternal beings living temporary experiences.

Jesus is the Christ, the Son of the living God. He lives, and because He lives, all of God's children will live forever. Thanks to His atoning sacrifice, we can all live together with Them. In the name of Jesus Christ, amen.

Notes

1. See Luke 10:27.
2. Russell M. Nelson, "Ministering," *Ensign* or *Liahona*, May 2018, 100.
3. John 13:35.
4. See 1 Kings 17:7.
5. See 1 Nephi 16:18.
6. Russell M. Nelson, "Joy and Spiritual Survival," *Ensign* or *Liahona*, Nov. 2016, 82.
7. See 1 Kings 17:10.
8. See 1 Nephi 16:23.
9. "A Child's Prayer," *Children's Songbook*, 12–13.
10. Moses 1:39.
12. Joseph Smith—History 1:17.
13. Matthew 26:39.

THIS DAY

ELDER RONALD A. RASBAND
Of the Quorum of the Twelve Apostles

My dear brothers and sisters, in the Book of Mormon the phrase "this day"[1] is used repeatedly to call attention to counsel, promises, and teachings. King Benjamin, in his final address, admonished the people, "Hear my words which I shall speak unto you this day; . . . open your ears that ye may hear, and your hearts that ye may understand, and your minds that the mysteries of God may be unfolded to your view."[2] General conference is a similar setting. We come to hear counsel for "this day," that we may be "true at all times"[3] to the Lord and His gospel. Pressing upon me "this day" is the importance of renewing our commitment to the Book of Mormon, which Joseph Smith called "the most correct of any book on earth."[4]

I hold in my hand a copy of the Book of Mormon. This is my 1970 vintage edition, and it is precious to me. By its appearance it is tired and worn, but no other book is as important to my life and my testimony as this one. Reading it, I gained a witness by the Spirit that Jesus Christ is the Son of God,[5] that He is my Savior,[6] that these scriptures are the word of God,[7] and that the gospel is restored.[8] Those truths rest deep within me. As the prophet Nephi said, "My soul delighteth in the things of the Lord."[9]

Here is the back story. As a young missionary, I took the counsel of Elder Marion D. Hanks, who visited us in the Eastern States Mission. He was the former president of the British Mission, and two of his missionaries are on the stand this day: my dear Brethren Elder Jeffrey R. Holland and Elder Quentin L. Cook.[10] Just as with his missionaries in England, he challenged us to read an unmarked copy of the Book of Mormon at least two times. I took up the task. The first reading I was to mark or underline everything that pointed to or testified of Jesus Christ. I used a red pencil, and I underlined many passages. The second time, Elder Hanks said to highlight principles and doctrine of the gospel, and this time I used blue to mark the scriptures. I read the Book of Mormon twice, as suggested, and then two more times, using yellow and black to mark passages that stood out to me.[11] I made many notations.

There was much more to my reading than just marking scriptures. With each reading of the Book of Mormon, front to back, I was filled with a profound love for the Lord. I felt a deeply rooted witness of the truth of His teachings and how they apply to "this day." This book fits its title, "Another Testament of Jesus Christ."[12] With that study and the spiritual witness that was received, I became a Book of Mormon missionary and a disciple of Jesus Christ.[13]

"This day," one of the greatest missionaries of the Book of Mormon is President Russell M. Nelson. When he was a newly called Apostle, he gave a lecture in Accra, Ghana.[14] In attendance were dignitaries, including an African tribal king, with whom he spoke through an interpreter. The king was a serious student of the Bible and loved the Lord. Following President Nelson's remarks, he was approached by that king, who asked in perfect English, "Just who are you?" President Nelson explained that he was an ordained Apostle of Jesus Christ.[15] The king's next question was "What can you teach me about Jesus Christ?"[16]

President Nelson reached for the Book of Mormon and opened it to 3 Nephi 11. Together President Nelson and the king read the Savior's sermon to the Nephites: "Behold, I am Jesus Christ, whom the prophets testified shall come into the world. . . . I am the light and the life of the world."[17]

President Nelson presented the king with that copy of the Book of Mormon, and the king responded, "You could have given me diamonds or rubies, but nothing is more precious to me than this additional knowledge about the Lord Jesus Christ."[18]

That is not an isolated example of how our beloved prophet shares the Book of Mormon. He has given copies of the Book of Mormon to hundreds of people, always bearing his witness of Jesus Christ. When President Nelson meets with guests, presidents, kings, heads of state, and leaders of business and organizations and of diverse faiths, whether at Church headquarters or in their own locations, he reverently presents this book of revealed scripture. He could give them so many things wrapped in ribbons that might sit on a table or desk or in cabinets as a reminder of his visit. Instead, he gives what is most precious to him, far beyond rubies and diamonds, as the tribal king described.

"The truths of the Book of Mormon," President Nelson has said, "have the *power* to heal, comfort, restore, succor, strengthen, console, and cheer our souls."[19] I have watched as these copies of the Book of Mormon have been clutched in the hands of those who have received them from our prophet of God. There could be no greater gift.

Just recently he met with the first lady of The Gambia in his office and humbly handed her a Book of Mormon. He did not stop there. He opened its pages to read with her, to teach and testify of Jesus Christ, His Atonement, and His love for all God's children—everywhere.

Our living prophet is doing his part to flood the earth with the Book of Mormon.[20] But he cannot open the floodgates alone. We must follow his lead.

Inspired by his example, I have been trying to humbly and more fervently share the Book of Mormon.

Recently I was on assignment in Mozambique. The citizens of this beautiful country are struggling with poverty, poor health, unemployment, storms, and political unrest. I had the honor of meeting with the country's president, Filipe Nyusi. At his request, I prayed for him and his nation; I told him we were building a temple of Jesus Christ[21] in his country. At the end of our visit, I presented to him a copy of the Book of Mormon in Portuguese, his native language. As he gratefully accepted the book, I testified of the hope and promise for his people, found in the Lord's words on its pages.[22]

On another occasion, my wife, Melanie, and I met with King Letsie III of Lesotho and his wife at their home.[23] For us, the highlight of our visit was presenting them with a copy of the Book of Mormon and then sharing my testimony. When I look back on that experience and others, a verse of latter-day scripture comes to mind:

"The fulness of my gospel might be proclaimed by the weak and the simple unto the ends of the world, and before kings and rulers."[24]

I have shared the Book of Mormon with India's Ambassador to the United Nations in Geneva, Indra Mani Pandey[25]; with His Holiness Patriarch Bartholomew[26] of the Eastern Orthodox Church; and with many others. I have felt the Spirit of the Lord with us as I have personally handed them this "keystone of our religion"[27] and borne my witness of Jesus Christ, the cornerstone of our faith.[28]

Now, brothers and sisters, you do not have to go to Mozambique or India or meet with kings and rulers to give someone this book of sacred teachings and promises. I invite you, this day, to give a Book of Mormon to your friends and family, your associates at work, your soccer coach, or the produce man at your market. They need the words of the Lord found in this book. They need answers to the questions of everyday life and of eternal life to come. They need to know of the covenant path laid out before them and the Lord's abiding love for them. It's all here in the Book of Mormon.

When you hand them a Book of Mormon, you are opening their minds and hearts to the word of God. You do not need to carry printed copies of the book with you. You can easily share it from your mobile phone from the scriptures section of the Gospel Library app.[29]

Think of all those who could be blessed by the gospel in their lives, and then send to them a copy of the Book of Mormon from your phone. Remember to include your testimony and how this book has blessed your life.

My dear friends, as an Apostle of the Lord, I invite you to follow our beloved prophet, President Nelson, in flooding the earth with the Book of Mormon. The need is so great; we need to act now. I promise that you will be participating in "*the greatest* work on earth," the gathering of Israel,[30] as you are inspired to reach out to those who have been "kept from the truth because they know not where to find it."[31] They need your testimony and witness of how this book has changed your life and drawn you closer to God, His peace,[32] and His "tidings of great joy."[33]

I testify that by divine design the Book of Mormon was prepared in ancient America to come forth to declare God's word, to bring souls to the Lord Jesus Christ and His restored gospel "this day." In the name of Jesus Christ, amen.

Notes

1. See Jacob 2:2–3; Mosiah 2:14, 30; 5:7; Alma 7:15; and many other verses in the Book of Mormon.
2. Mosiah 2:9.
3. Alma 53:20.
4. *Teachings of Presidents of the Church: Joseph Smith* (2007), 64. The full statement given by Joseph Smith on November 28, 1841, in council with the Twelve Apostles: "I told the brethren that the Book of Mormon was the most correct of any book on earth, and the keystone of our religion, and a man would get nearer to God by abiding by its precepts, than by any other book." The key reference to "correct" can be attributed to revelation received in the book's translation and the doctrine taught in the Book of Mormon that establishes better than any other book the "plain and precious" truths of the gospel (see 1 Nephi 13:40).
5. See "The Living Christ: The Testimony of the Apostles," a declaration by the First Presidency and Quorum of the Twelve Apostles, January 1, 2000: "We bear testimony, as His duly ordained Apostles—that Jesus is the Living Christ, the immortal Son of God. He is the great King Immanuel, who stands today on the right hand of His Father. He is the light, the life, and the hope of the world. His way is the path that leads to happiness in this life and eternal life in the world to come. God be thanked for the matchless gift of His divine Son" (ChurchofJesusChrist.org).
6. See Isaiah 49:26; 1 Nephi 21:26; 22:12; Doctrine and Covenants 66:1.
7. The word of God is found in the scriptures. For example, in the Book of Mormon, Laman and Lemuel questioned, "What meaneth the rod of iron?" referring to Lehi's dream. Nephi responded, "It was the word of God; and whoso would hearken unto the word of God, and would hold fast unto it, they would never perish; neither could the temptations and the fiery darts of the adversary overpower them unto blindness, to lead them away to destruction" (1 Nephi 15:23–24).
8. See "The Restoration of the Fulness of the Gospel of Jesus Christ: A Bicentennial Proclamation to the World," which includes the following: "We declare that The Church of Jesus Christ of Latter-day Saints, organized on April 6, 1830, is Christ's New Testament Church restored. This Church is anchored in the perfect life of its chief cornerstone, Jesus Christ, and in His infinite Atonement and literal Resurrection. Jesus Christ has once again called Apostles and has given them priesthood authority. He invites all of us to come unto Him and His Church, to receive the Holy Ghost, the ordinances of salvation, and to gain enduring joy. . . . We gladly declare that the promised Restoration goes forward through continuing revelation. The earth will never again be the same, as God will 'gather together in one all things in Christ' (Ephesians 1:10)" (ChurchofJesusChrist.org).
9. 2 Nephi 4:16.
10. See Quentin L. Cook, "Be Not Weary in Well-Doing" (Brigham Young University devotional, Aug. 24, 2020), speeches.byu.edu; Eliza Smith-Driggs, "This Week on Social: How to Develop a Love for the Lord, Yourself and Others," *Church News*, July 17, 2020, thechurchnews.com.
11. Third reading, yellow: geology or geography; fourth reading, black: storyline of the Book of Mormon.
12. "Another Testament of Jesus Christ" was added as a subtitle to all editions of the Book of Mormon. Church leaders made the name change to further emphasize the purpose of the book as stated on the title page: "And also to the convincing of the Jew and Gentile that Jesus is the Christ, the Eternal God, manifesting himself unto all nations."
13. Being a disciple of Jesus Christ is an expression of our love for Him. Disciples have been baptized; they take upon themselves the name of Jesus Christ; they strive to follow Him by embracing His attributes as described by the Apostle Peter: "Giving all diligence, add to your faith

virtue; and to virtue knowledge; and to knowledge temperance; and to temperance patience; and to patience godliness; and to godliness brotherly kindness; and to brotherly kindness charity" (2 Peter 1:5–7; see also *Preach My Gospel: A Guide to Missionary Service* [2019], 121–32).

14. President Russell M. Nelson, an internationally known heart surgeon before his call to the Quorum of the Twelve Apostles in 1984, gave a lecture at a medical school in Accra, Ghana, in 1986 on the history of heart surgery. Interviewed later by the media, he explained he was there "as a servant of the Lord to help [the people] become better citizens, to build strong families, to gain true happiness and prosper in the land." He returned to Accra, Ghana, on November 16, 2001, for the groundbreaking of the Accra Ghana Temple (see "Ground Broken for First Temple in West Africa," *Church News*, Nov. 24, 2001, thechurchnews.com).

15. See *General Handbook: Serving in The Church of Jesus Christ of Latter-day Saints*, 5.1.1.1: "In our day, the Lord calls men through the President of the Church to be ordained as Apostles and to serve in the Quorum of the Twelve Apostles (see Doctrine and Covenants 18:26–28)" (ChurchofJesusChrist.org).

16. See Russell M. Nelson, "The Book of Mormon: What Would Your Life Be Like without It?," *Ensign* or *Liahona*, Nov. 2017, 60.

17. 3 Nephi 11:10–11.

18. See Russell M. Nelson, "The Book of Mormon: What Would Your Life Be Like without It?," 61.

19. Russell M. Nelson, "The Book of Mormon: What Would Your Life Be Like without It?," 62.

20. See Moses 7:62.

21. The Beira Mozambique Temple was announced on April 4, 2021, by President Russell M. Nelson. More than half a million people live in Beira, which lies on the coast of the Indian Ocean.

22. Examples of the hope and promises found in the Book of Mormon include 2 Nephi 31:20; Jacob 4:4–6; Alma 13:28–29; 22:16; 34:41; Ether 12:32; Moroni 7:41; 8:26.

23. Elder and Sister Rasband met with the royal family on February 10, 2020, when on assignment in Africa to dedicate the Durban South Africa Temple.

24. Doctrine and Covenants 1:23.

25. Elder Rasband met with Ambassador Indra Mani Pandey, Permanent Representative of India to the United Nations and Other International Organizations in Geneva, while on assignment to the Interfaith Forum in Bologna, Italy, on September 17, 2021.

26. Elder Rasband met with His All Holiness Ecumenical Patriarch Bartholomew of the Eastern Orthodox Church while on assignment to the Interfaith Forum in Bologna, Italy, on September 13, 2021.

27. *Teachings: Joseph Smith*, 64. A keystone is a wedge-shaped piece of masonry that sits at the crown of an arch, holding the other pieces in place. The Prophet Joseph described the Book of Mormon as "the keystone of our religion" because of its importance in uniting the Church through principles and ordinances. The Book of Mormon serves as a "keystone" for the lives of members, helping them stay firmly on the covenant path.

28. See Ephesians 2:19–20. Jesus Christ is the chief cornerstone of our Church, which bears His name. Just as the laying of a cornerstone at the temple is symbolic of the main stone forming the corner of the foundation of God's house, Jesus Christ is the cornerstone of our faith and our salvation. He gave His life that we might live; there is none equal to Him in strength, in purpose, or in love.

29. You can share it from your mobile phone. One way is by opening the Gospel Library app, going to the "Scriptures" collection, and then tapping "Share Now" at the top. Or from within the Book of Mormon app, you can tap the "Share" icon, which displays a digital code that a friend can easily scan using his or her phone.

30. Russell M. Nelson, "Hope of Israel" (worldwide youth devotional, June 3, 2018), HopeofIsrael .ChurchofJesusChrist.org. "On June 3, 2018, President Russell M. Nelson and his wife, Wendy W. Nelson, invited the youth to 'enlist in the youth battalion of the Lord' and take part in '*the greatest* challenge, *the greatest* cause, and *the greatest* work on earth.' And what is the greatest challenge? The gathering of Israel" (Charlotte Larcabal, "A Call to Enlist and Gather Israel," *New Era*, Mar. 2019, 24).

31. Doctrine and Covenants 123:12.

32. See 2 Nephi 4:27; Mosiah 4:3; 15:18; Alma 46:12.

33. 1 Nephi 13:37.

WHAT IS TRUE?

PRESIDENT RUSSELL M. NELSON

President of The Church of Jesus Christ of Latter-day Saints

My beloved brothers and sisters, thanks to all for this inspiring session! Since our conference last April, we have witnessed many world events, ranging from the heartbreaking to the sublime.

We are delighted with reports of large youth conferences being held throughout the world.[1] At these conferences, our noble youth are learning that no matter what happens in their lives, their greatest strength comes from the Lord.[2]

We rejoice that more temples are being built across the world. With the dedication of each new temple, additional godly power comes into the world to strengthen us and counteracts the intensifying efforts of the adversary.

Abuse constitutes the influence of the adversary. It is a grievous sin.[3] As President of the Church, I affirm the teachings of the Lord Jesus Christ on this issue. Let me be perfectly clear: *any* kind of abuse of women, children, or anyone is an abomination to the Lord. He grieves and *I grieve* whenever *anyone* is harmed. He mourns and *we all mourn* for each person who has fallen victim to abuse of any kind. Those who perpetrate these hideous acts are not only accountable to the laws of man but will also face the wrath of Almighty God.

For decades now, the Church has taken extensive measures to protect—in particular—children from abuse. There are many aids on the Church website. I invite you to study them.[4] These guidelines are in place to protect the innocent. I urge each of us to be alert to anyone who might be in danger of being abused and to act promptly to protect them. The Savior will not tolerate abuse, and as His disciples, neither can we.

The adversary has other disturbing tactics. Among them are his efforts to blur the line between what is true and what is not true. The flood of information available at our fingertips, ironically, makes it increasingly difficult to determine what is true.

This challenge reminds me of an experience Sister Nelson and I had when we visited a dignitary in a country where relatively few people have heard of Jesus Christ. This dear aging friend had recently been quite ill. He told us that during his many days in bed, he often stared at the ceiling and asked, "What is true?"

Many on earth today "are only kept from the truth because they know not where to find it."[5] Some would have us believe that truth is relative—that each person should determine for himself or herself what is true. Such a belief is but wishful thinking for those who mistakenly think they will not also be accountable to God.

Dear brothers and sisters, God is the source of all truth. The Church of Jesus Christ of Latter-day Saints embraces *all* truth that God conveys to His children, whether learned in a scientific laboratory or received by direct revelation from Him.

From this pulpit today and tomorrow, you will continue to hear truth. Please make notes of thoughts that catch your attention and those that come into your mind and stay in your heart. Prayerfully ask the Lord to confirm that what you have heard is true.

I love you, my dear brothers and sisters. I pray that this conference will provide the spiritual feast you are seeking. In the sacred name of Jesus Christ, amen.

Notes

1. Known as For the Strength of Youth, or FSY, conferences.
2. The guidebook *For the Strength of Youth* has recently been revised.
3. See Matthew 18:6; Doctrine and Covenants 121:34–37.
4. See abuse.ChurchofJesusChrist.org.
5. Doctrine and Covenants 123:12.

SATURDAY AFTERNOON SESSION

OCTOBER 1, 2022

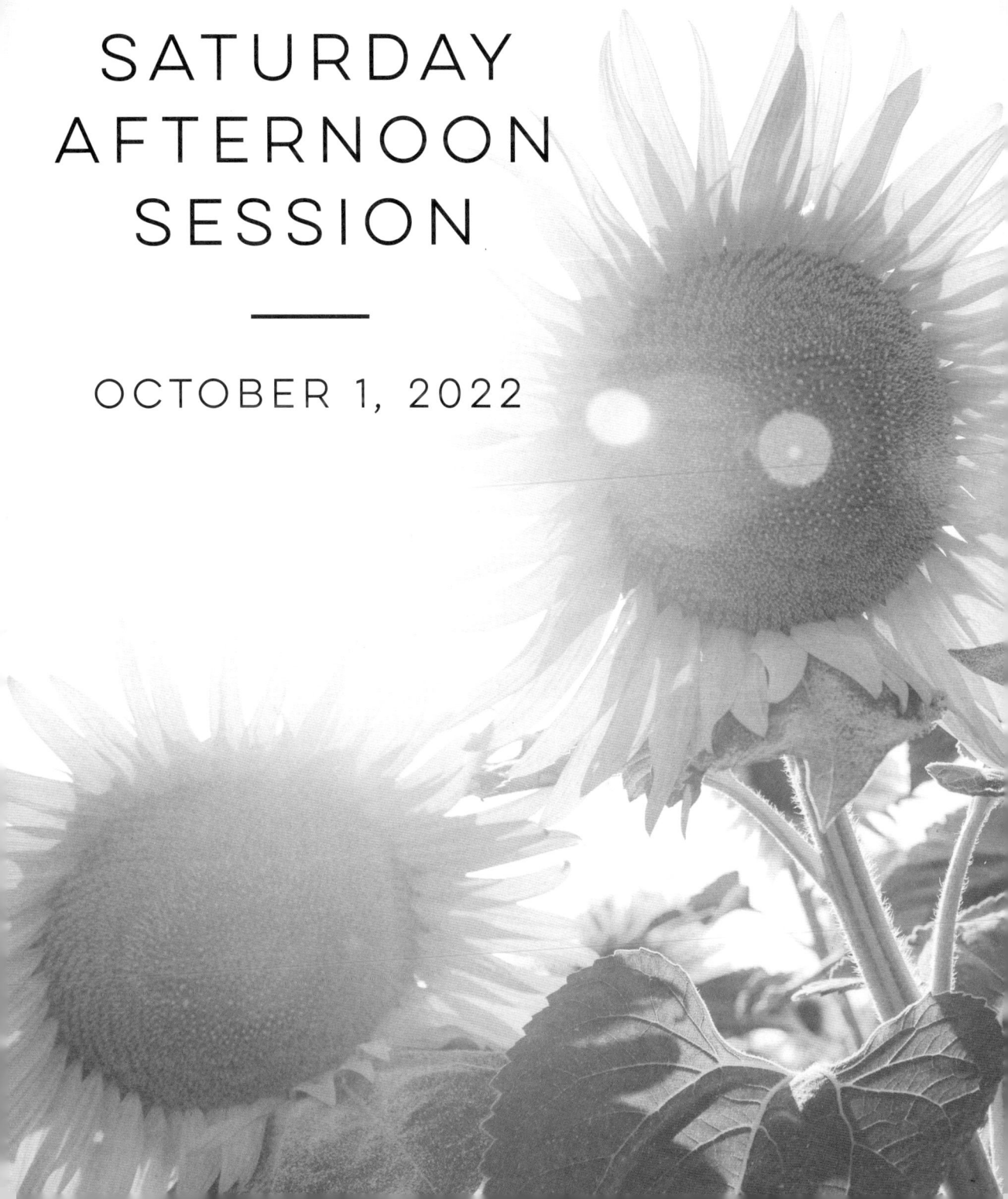

FOLLOW JESUS CHRIST WITH FOOTSTEPS OF FAITH

PRESIDENT M. RUSSELL BALLARD

Acting President of the Quorum of the Twelve Apostles

Thank you, choir, for singing "Faith in Every Footstep." The music and words of that song were written in 1996 by Brother Newell Dayley[1] in preparation for the celebration of the 150th anniversary of the arrival of the early pioneers to the Salt Lake Valley in 1847.

Although this song was written in preparation for that celebration, its message applies to the whole world.

I have always loved the chorus:

> *With faith in ev'ry footstep, we follow Christ, the Lord;*
> *And filled with hope through his pure love, we sing with*
> *one accord.*[2]

Brothers and sisters, I testify that as we follow Jesus Christ with footsteps of faith, there is hope. There is hope in the Lord Jesus Christ. There is hope for all in this life. There is hope to overcome our mistakes, our sorrows, our struggles, and our trials and our troubles. There is hope in repentance and being forgiven and in forgiving others. I testify that there is hope and peace in Christ. He can carry us today through difficult times. He did it for the early pioneers, and He will do it now for each one of us.

This year marks the 175th anniversary of the arrival of the early pioneers to the Salt Lake Valley, which has caused me to reflect on my ancestors, some of whom walked from Nauvoo to the Salt Lake Valley. I have great-grandparents who walked the plains in their youth. Henry Ballard was 20 years old;[3] Margaret McNeil was 13;[4] and Joseph F. Smith, who later became the sixth President of the Church, was just 9 when he arrived in the Salt Lake Valley.[5]

They faced deprivations of every kind along the trail, such as cold winters, illness, and lack of adequate food and clothing. For instance, when Henry Ballard entered the Salt Lake Valley, he rejoiced in seeing the "Promised Land" but lived in fear that someone might see him because the clothing he was wearing was so worn out that it did not completely cover his body. He hid himself behind bushes all day until after dark. He then went to a house and begged for clothing so that he could continue his journey and locate his parents. He was thankful to God that he had reached his future home in safety.[6]

My great-grandparents followed Jesus Christ with footsteps of faith throughout each of their trials. I am grateful to them for never giving up. Their footsteps of faith have blessed me and subsequent generations, just as your footsteps of faith today will bless your posterity.

The word *pioneer* is both a noun and a verb. As a noun it can mean a person who is among the first to explore or settle a new territory. As a verb, it can mean to open or prepare the way for others to follow.[7]

As I think about pioneers who have prepared the way for others, I first think of the Prophet Joseph Smith. Joseph was a pioneer because his footsteps of faith led him to a grove of trees, where he knelt in prayer and opened the way for us to have the fulness of the gospel of Jesus Christ. Joseph's faith to "ask of God"[8] on that spring morning in 1820 opened the way for the Restoration of the fulness of the gospel of Jesus Christ, which included prophets and apostles called to serve on earth once again.[9] I know Joseph Smith is a prophet of God. I know his faith-filled footsteps led him to kneel in the presence of God the Father and His Beloved Son, Jesus Christ.

The Prophet Joseph's footsteps of faith enabled him to be the Lord's instrument in bringing forth the Book of Mormon, which is another testament of Jesus Christ and His atoning grace.

Through Joseph Smith's faith and perseverance in the face of incredible hardship and opposition, he was able to be an instrument in the hands of the Lord in establishing the Church of Jesus Christ once again on the earth.

During the last general conference, I spoke about how my full-time missionary service blessed me. I was blessed as I taught about our Heavenly Father's glorious plan of salvation, Joseph Smith's First Vision, and his translation of the Book of Mormon. These restored teachings and doctrine guided my footsteps of faith in teaching those who were willing to listen to the message of the Restoration of the gospel.

Our missionaries today are modern-day pioneers because they share this glorious message with people around the world, thus opening the way for our Heavenly Father's children to know Him and His Son, Jesus Christ. Accepting the gospel of Jesus Christ opens the way for everyone to prepare for and receive ordinances and the blessings of the Church and the temple.

Last general conference, President Russell M. Nelson reaffirmed "that the Lord has asked every worthy, able young man to prepare for and serve a mission" and that "a mission is also a powerful, but optional, opportunity" for "young and able sisters."[10]

Dear young men and young women, your footsteps of faith will help you to follow the Lord's invitation to serve missions—to be modern-day pioneers—by opening the way for God's children to find and stay on the covenant path leading back to His glorious presence.

President Nelson has been a pioneer in the Church. As an Apostle he has traveled to and opened many lands for the preaching of the gospel. Shortly after becoming the prophet and President of the Church, he pled with us to "increase [our] spiritual capacity to receive revelation."[11] He continues to teach us to strengthen our testimonies. In a devotional for young adults, he said:

"I plead with you to take charge of your testimony. Work for it. Own it. Care for it. Nurture it so that it will grow. . . .

"[Then] watch for miracles to happen in your life."[12]

He is teaching us how to become more spiritually self-reliant. He has said that "in coming days, it will not be possible to survive spiritually without the guiding, directing, comforting, and constant influence of the Holy Ghost."[13]

I testify that President Russell M. Nelson is the prophet of God on the earth today.

Our Savior, Jesus Christ, is the ultimate pioneer in preparing the way. Indeed, He *is* "the way"[14] for the plan of salvation to be accomplished so that we can repent and, through faith in Him, return to our Heavenly Father.

Jesus said, "I am the way, the truth, and the life: no man cometh unto the Father, but by me."[15] He has promised to not leave us comfortless; He will come to us in our trials.[16] He has invited us to "come unto [Him] with full purpose of heart, and [He] shall heal [us]."[17]

I testify that Jesus Christ is our Savior and our Redeemer, our Advocate with the Father. Our Heavenly Father has opened the way for us to return to Him by following His Beloved Son, Jesus Christ, with faith in every footstep.

My great-grandparents and other early pioneers faced many obstacles as they came by wagons, handcarts, and walking to the Salt Lake Valley. We too will face challenges in our individual journeys through our lives. We are not pushing handcarts or driving covered wagons over steep mountains and through deep snowdrifts; we are trying as they did to spiritually overcome the temptations and challenges of our day. We have trails to walk; we have hills—and sometimes mountains—to climb. Although the trials today are different than those of the early pioneers, they are no less challenging for us.

It is important to follow the prophet and keep our feet firmly planted on the covenant path of faithfulness, as it was for the early pioneers.

Let us follow Jesus Christ with faith in every footstep. We need to serve the Lord and serve one another. We need to strengthen ourselves spiritually by keeping and honoring our covenants. We should not lose the sense of urgency to keep the commandments. Satan tries to dull our commitment and our love for God and the Lord Jesus Christ. Please remember that if anyone should lose their way, we will never be lost to our Savior. With the blessing of repentance, we can turn to Him. He will help us learn, grow, and change as we strive to stay on the covenant path.

May we ever follow in the footsteps of Jesus Christ and, with faith in our every footstep, focus on Him, keeping our feet firmly planted on the covenant path, is my humble prayer in the name of Jesus Christ, amen.

Notes

1. See K. Newell Dayley, "Faith in Every Footstep," *Ensign*, Jan. 1997, 15; *Liahona*, Feb. 1997, 22–23.
2. Dayley, "Faith in Every Footstep," *Ensign*, Jan. 1997, 15; *Liahona*, Feb. 1997, 23.
3. See Henry Ballard diary, L. Tom Perry Special Collections, Harold B. Lee Library, Brigham Young University, Provo, Utah, archives.lib.byu.edu/repositories/ltpsc/resources/upb_msssc998.
4. See "A 'Small Glimpse' into Pioneer Experiences," *Church News*, June 15, 1996, thechurchnews .com.
5. See *Teachings of Presidents of the Church: Joseph F. Smith* (1998), xiv.
6. See Douglas O. Crookston, ed., *Henry Ballard: The Story of a Courageous Pioneer, 1832–1908* (1994), 14–15.
7. See *Merriam-Webster.com Dictionary*, "pioneer."
8. James 1:5.
9. See Joseph Smith—History 1:5–20.
10. Russell M. Nelson, "Preaching the Gospel of Peace," *Liahona*, May 2022, 6; original emphasis removed.
11. Russell M. Nelson, "Revelation for the Church, Revelation for Our Lives," *Ensign* or *Liahona*, May 2018, 96.
12. Russell M. Nelson, "Choices for Eternity" (worldwide devotional for young adults, May 15, 2022), broadcasts.ChurchofJesusChrist.org.
13. Russell M. Nelson, "Revelation for the Church, Revelation for Our Lives," 96.
14. John 14:6.
15. John 14:6.
16. See John 14:16–18.
17. 3 Nephi 18:32.

BEAUTY FOR ASHES: THE HEALING PATH OF FORGIVENESS

SISTER KRISTIN M. YEE

Second Counselor in the Relief Society General Presidency

The book of 1 Samuel includes a lesser-known story of David, the future king of Israel, and a woman named Abigail.

After Samuel's death, David and his men went away from King Saul, who sought David's life. They provided watchcare for the flocks and servants of a wealthy man named Nabal, who was mean-spirited. David sent 10 of his men to salute Nabal and request much-needed food and supplies.

Nabal responded to David's request with insult and sent his men away empty-handed.

Offended, David prepared his men to go up against Nabal and his household, saying, "He hath requited me evil for good."[1] A servant told Abigail, Nabal's wife, about her husband's ill treatment of David's men. Abigail quickly gathered the needed food and supplies and went to intercede.

When Abigail met him, she "fell before David on her face, and bowed herself to the ground,

"And fell at his feet, and said, Upon me, my lord, upon me let this iniquity be. . . .

"Now therefore, . . . the Lord hath withholden thee from coming to shed blood, and from avenging thyself with thine own hand. . . .

". . . Now this blessing which thine handmaid hath brought unto my lord, let it even be given unto the young men. . . .

"I pray thee, forgive the trespass of thine handmaid. . . .

"And David said to Abigail, Blessed be the Lord God of Israel, which sent thee this day to meet me:

"And blessed be thy advice, and blessed be thou, which hast kept me this day from coming to shed blood, and from avenging myself with mine own hand. . . .

"So David received of her hand that which she had brought

him, and said unto her, Go up in peace to thine house; . . . I have hearkened to thy voice, and have accepted thy person."[2]

They both departed in peace.

In this account, Abigail can be seen as a powerful type or symbol of Jesus Christ.[3] Through His atoning sacrifice, He can release us from the sin and weight of a warring heart and provide us with the sustenance we need.[4]

Just as Abigail was willing to take Nabal's sin upon herself, so did the Savior—in an incomprehensible way—take upon Him our sins and the sins of those who have hurt or offended us.[5] In Gethsemane and on the cross, He claimed these sins. He made a way for us to let go of a vengeful heart. That "way" is through forgiving—which can be one of the most difficult things we ever do and one of the most divine things we ever experience. On the path of forgiveness, Jesus Christ's atoning power can flow into our lives and begin to heal the deep crevasses of the heart and soul.

President Russell M. Nelson has taught that the Savior offers us the ability to forgive:

"Through His infinite Atonement, you can forgive those who have hurt you and who may never accept responsibility for their cruelty to you.

"It is usually easy to forgive one who sincerely and humbly seeks your forgiveness. But the Savior will grant you the ability to forgive anyone who has mistreated you in any way. Then their hurtful acts can no longer canker your soul."[6]

Abigail's bringing an abundance of food and supplies can teach us that the Savior offers to those who have been hurt and injured the sustenance and help we need to be healed and made whole.[7] We are not left to deal with the consequences of others' actions on our own; we too can be made whole and given the chance to be saved from the weight of a warring heart and any actions that may follow.

The Lord has said, "I, the Lord, will forgive whom I will forgive, but of you it is required to forgive all men."[8] The Lord requires us to forgive for our own good.[9] But He does not ask us to do it without His help, His love, His understanding. Through our covenants with the Lord, we can each receive the strengthening power, guidance, and the help we need to both forgive and to be forgiven.

Please know that forgiving someone does not mean that you put yourself in a position where you will continue to be hurt. "We can work toward forgiving someone and still feel prompted by the Spirit to stay away from them."[10]

Just as Abigail helped David not to have an "offence of heart"[11] and to receive the help he needed, so will the Savior help you. He loves you, and He is meeting you on your path "with healing in His wings."[12] He desires your peace.

I have personally witnessed the miracle of Christ healing my warring heart. With permission of my father, I share that I grew up in a home where I didn't always feel safe because of emotional and verbal mistreatment. In my youth and young adult years, I resented my father and had anger in my heart from that hurt.

Over the years and in my efforts to find peace and healing on the path of forgiveness, I came to realize in a profound way that the same Son of God who atoned for my sins is the same Redeemer who will also save those who have deeply hurt me. I could not truly believe the first truth without believing the second.

As my love for the Savior has grown, so has my desire to replace hurt and anger with His healing balm. It has been a process of many years, requiring courage, vulnerability, perseverance, and learning to trust in the Savior's divine power to save and heal. I still have work to do, but my heart is no longer on a warpath. I have been given "a new heart"[13]—one that has felt the deep and abiding love of a personal Savior, who stayed beside me, who gently and patiently led me to a better place, who wept with me, who knew my sorrow.

The Lord has sent me compensatory blessings just as Abigail brought what David needed. He has sent mentors into my life. And sweetest and most transformative of all has been my relationship with my Heavenly Father. Through Him, I've gratefully known the gentle, protective, and guiding love of a perfect Father.

Elder Richard G. Scott said: "You cannot erase what has been done, but you can forgive.[14] Forgiveness heals terrible, tragic wounds, for it allows the love of God to purge your heart and mind of the poison of hate. It cleanses your consciousness of the desire for revenge. It makes place for the purifying, healing, restoring love of the Lord."[15]

My earthly father has also had a miraculous change of heart in recent years and has turned to the Lord—something I wouldn't have anticipated in this life. Another testimony to me of the complete and transformative power of Jesus Christ.

I know He is able to heal the sinner and those sinned against. He is the Savior and the Redeemer of the world, who laid down His life that we might live again. He said, "The Spirit of the Lord is upon me, because he hath anointed me to preach the gospel to the poor; he hath sent me to *heal the brokenhearted*, to preach deliverance to the captives, and recovering of sight to the blind, to *set at liberty them that are bruised*."[16]

To all who are brokenhearted, captive, bruised, and perhaps blinded by hurt or sin, He offers healing, recovery, and deliverance. I testify that that healing and recovery He offers is real. The timing of that healing is individual, and we cannot judge another's timing. It is important to allow ourselves the necessary time to heal and to be kind to ourselves in the process. The Savior is ever merciful and attentive and stands ready to provide the succor we need.[17]

On the path of forgiveness and healing lies a choice not to perpetuate unhealthy patterns or relationships in our families or elsewhere. To all within our influence, we can offer kindness for cruelty, love for hate, gentleness for abrasiveness, safety for distress, and peace for contention.

To give what you have been denied is a powerful part of divine healing possible through faith in Jesus Christ. To live in such a way that you give, as Isaiah has said, beauty for the ashes of your life[18] is an act of faith that follows the supreme example of a Savior who suffered all that He might succor all.

Joseph of Egypt lived a life with ashes. He was hated by his brethren, betrayed, sold into slavery, wrongly imprisoned, and forgotten by someone who had promised to help. Yet he trusted in the Lord.

"The Lord was with Joseph"[19] and consecrated his trials to his own blessing and growth—and to the saving of his family and all Egypt.

When Joseph met his brothers as a great leader in Egypt, his forgiveness and refined perspective were manifest in the gracious words he spoke:

"Now therefore be not grieved, nor angry with yourselves, that ye sold me hither: for God did send me before you to preserve life. . . .

"So now it was not you that sent me hither, but God."[20]

Through the Savior, Joseph's life became "beauty for ashes."[21]

Kevin J Worthen, president of BYU, has said that God "can make good come . . . not just from our successes but also from our failures and the failures of others that cause us pain. God is that good and that powerful."[22]

I testify that the greatest example of love and forgiveness is that of our Savior, Jesus Christ, who in bitter agony said, "Father, forgive them; for they know not what they do."[23]

I know that our Father in Heaven desires goodness and hope for each of His children. In Jeremiah we read, "For I know the thoughts that I think toward you, saith the Lord, thoughts of peace."[24]

Jesus Christ is your personal Messiah, your loving Redeemer and Savior, who knows the pleadings of your heart. He desires your healing and happiness. He loves you. He weeps with you in your sorrows and rejoices to make you whole. May we take heart and take His loving hand that is ever extended[25] as we walk the healing path of forgiveness is my prayer in the name of Jesus Christ, amen.

Notes

1. 1 Samuel 25:21.
2. 1 Samuel 25:23–24, 26–28, 32–33, 35.
3. See *Old Testament Seminary Student Material* (2018), 449–50.
4. See James L. Ferrell, *The Peacegiver: How Christ Offers to Heal Our Hearts and Homes* (2004), 29.
5. See *Old Testament Seminary Student Material*, 449–50.
6. Russell M. Nelson, "Four Gifts That Jesus Christ Offers to You" (First Presidency's Christmas devotional, Dec. 7, 2018), broadcasts.ChurchofJesusChrist.org.
7. See Ferrell, *The Peacegiver*, 53.
8. Doctrine and Covenants 64:10.
9. See James E. Faust, "The Healing Power of Forgiveness," *Ensign* or *Liahona*, May 2007, 67–69.
10. "Forgiveness Doesn't Mean Putting Up with Getting Hurt," Mar. 16, 2022, ChurchofJesusChrist .org.
11. 1 Samuel 25:31.
12. Malachi 4:2.

13. Ezekiel 36:26.
14. See Doctrine and Covenants 64:10.
15. Richard G. Scott, "Healing the Tragic Scars of Abuse," *Ensign*, May 1992, 33.
16. Luke 4:18; emphasis added.
17. See Alma 7:11–12.
18. See Isaiah 61:3.
19. Genesis 39:2, 21.
20. Genesis 45:5, 8.
21. Isaiah 61:3.
22. Kevin J Worthen, "The Y on the Mountain" (Brigham Young University commencement address, Apr. 25, 2019), 3, speeches.byu.edu.
23. Luke 23:34.
24. Jeremiah 29:11.
25. See Jacob 6:5.

BE PERFECTED IN HIM

ELDER PAUL V. JOHNSON
Of the Presidency of the Seventy

Our Heavenly Father and our Savior, Jesus Christ, have the power to save us and transform us. They can help us become as They are.

A few years ago, one of our young grandsons, Aaron, began having health problems. He became fatigued, had quite a bit of bruising, and did not look healthy. After medical testing, he was diagnosed with severe aplastic anemia, a disease where his bone marrow stopped producing red blood cells, white blood cells, and platelets. Without treatment and an eventual cure, his blood could not clot properly or fight off infections, so even minor falls, injuries, or illnesses could quickly become life-threatening.

For a period of time, Aaron received regular platelet and blood transfusions to keep him out of danger. The doctors explained that the only cure for the disease would be a bone marrow transplant, and the best chance for success would be to have a sibling as the donor. If one of his siblings were an ideal match, the outcome of the transplant could be lifesaving. His four younger brothers were tested, and one, Maxwell, was deemed a perfect match.

Even with a perfect donor match, a bone marrow transplant still poses a serious risk of complications. The process required that Aaron's own cells in his diseased bone marrow be destroyed by a combination of chemotherapy and radiation before receiving the stem cells from his brother Maxwell's bone marrow. Then because of Aaron's compromised immune system, he needed to be isolated in the hospital for several weeks and then at home for several months with special protocols, restrictions, and medications.

The hoped-for outcome from the transplant was that Aaron's body would not reject the donor cells and that Maxwell's cells would gradually produce the needed red and white blood cells and platelets in Aaron's body. A successful donor transplant causes a very real physiological change. Amazingly, a doctor explained that if Aaron committed a crime and left blood at the crime scene, the police

53

could arrest his brother Maxwell. This is because Aaron's blood would come from Maxwell's transplanted cells and have Maxwell's DNA, and this would be the case for the rest of his life.

Aaron being saved by his brother's blood has spurred many thoughts about the atoning blood of Jesus Christ and the effect of His Atonement on us. I would like to focus today on the permanent, life-giving change that occurs as we allow the Lord to work miracles in us.[1]

Aaron did not have the power in himself to overcome the disease. His body could not make the blood cells needed to sustain his life. No matter what he personally did, he could not heal his bone marrow. Just as Aaron could not cure himself, we cannot save ourselves. No matter how capable, educated, brilliant, or strong we are, we cannot cleanse ourselves from our sins, change our bodies to an immortal state, or exalt ourselves. It is only possible through the Savior Jesus Christ and His infinite Atonement. "There is none other way nor name given under heaven whereby man can be saved in the kingdom of God."[2] It is His atoning blood that cleanses us and sanctifies us.[3]

Although Aaron could not heal himself, in order for the transplant to work he needed to be willing to do what the doctors asked—even very difficult, challenging things. Although we can't save ourselves, when we submit to the Lord's will and keep our covenants, the way is open for our redemption.[4] Like the remarkable process of the very DNA of Aaron's blood cells changing, we can have our hearts changed,[5] have His image in our countenances,[6] and become new creatures in Christ.[7]

Alma reminded the people of Zarahemla of the previous generation that had been converted. Speaking of his father, Alma explained that "according to his faith there was a mighty change wrought in his heart."[8] He then asked, "Have ye experienced this mighty change in your hearts?"[9] It wasn't the people who changed their own hearts. The Lord performed the actual change. Alma was very clear about this. He said, "Behold, he changed their hearts."[10] They "humbled themselves and put their trust in the true and living God . . . [and]

were faithful until the end . . . [and] were saved."[11] The people were willing to open their hearts and exercise faith, and then the Lord changed their hearts. And what a mighty change it was! Think of the difference in the lives of these two men named Alma before and after their hearts were changed.[12]

We are children of God with a majestic destiny. We can be changed to become like Him and have "a fulness of joy."[13] Satan, on the other hand, would have us be miserable like he is.[14] We have the ability to choose whom we follow.[15] When we follow Satan, we give him power.[16] When we follow God, He gives us power.

The Savior taught that we "should be perfect."[17] This can seem so daunting. I can clearly see my personal inadequacies and am painfully aware of the distance between me and perfection. We may have a tendency to think we have to perfect ourselves, but that is not possible. Following every suggestion in every self-help book in the world will not bring it about. There is only one way and one name whereby perfection comes. We are "made perfect through Jesus the mediator of the new covenant, who wrought out this perfect atonement through the shedding of his own blood."[18] Our perfection is only possible through God's grace.

Can you imagine how overwhelming it would have been for our young grandson Aaron to assume he had to understand and perform all the medical procedures associated with his transplant himself? We should not assume we need to do what only the Savior can do in the miraculous process of our perfection.

As Moroni concluded his record, he taught, "Yea, come unto Christ, and be perfected in him, . . . and if ye shall deny yourselves of all ungodliness, and love God with all your might, mind and strength, then is his grace sufficient for you, that by his grace ye may be perfect in Christ."[19] What a comforting and powerful truth! His grace is sufficient for me. His grace is sufficient for you. His grace is sufficient for all who "labour and are heavy laden."[20]

With medical treatments like Aaron's, there is always some uncertainty of the outcome. In fact, Aaron needed a second transplant when the first one had complications. Thankfully, with a spiritual change of heart, we don't have to wonder if it will happen. When we live according to His will, "relying wholly upon the merits of him who is mighty to save,"[21] there is a 100 percent guarantee of being cleansed by the Savior's blood and eventually being perfected in Him. He is "a God of truth, and [cannot] lie."[22]

There is no question that this process of change takes time and will not be completed until after this life, but the promise is sure. When the fulfillment of God's promises seems far off, we still embrace those promises, knowing they will be fulfilled.[23]

The miraculous change in Aaron's health has brought great joy to our family. Imagine the great joy in heaven as mighty changes happen in our souls.

Our Heavenly Father and our Savior, Jesus Christ, love us and have graciously offered to change us and perfect us. They want to do this. It is central to Their work and glory.[24] I testify They have power to do this as we come to Them in faith. In the name of Jesus Christ, amen.

Notes

1. See Alma 23:6.
2. 2 Nephi 31:21.
3. See 1 Peter 1:18–19; Revelation 1:5; Moses 6:59–60.
4. See 3 Nephi 18:1–12; 27:20; Doctrine and Covenants 132:19.
5. See Alma 5:7.
6. See Alma 5:14.
7. See Mosiah 27:25–27.
8. Alma 5:12.
9. Alma 5:14.
10. Alma 5:7.
11. Alma 5:13.
12. See Mosiah 18:1–3; 27:8–10; Alma 4:15–20.
13. Doctrine and Covenants 93:33.
14. See 2 Nephi 2:18.
15. See 2 Nephi 2:27.
16. See 2 Nephi 26:22; 28:22; Mosiah 16:5; Alma 34:39; 3 Nephi 7:5; Doctrine and Covenants 29:40.
17. 3 Nephi 12:48.
18. Doctrine and Covenants 76:69.
19. Moroni 10:32.
20. Matthew 11:28.
21. 2 Nephi 31:19.
22. Ether 3:12.
23. See Hebrews 11:13.
24. See Moses 1:39.

IN PARTNERSHIP WITH THE LORD

ELDER ULISSES SOARES
Of the Quorum of the Twelve Apostles

Within the first few months of our marriage, my dear wife expressed her desire to study music. Intending to please her, I decided to orchestrate a big, heartfelt surprise for my sweetheart. I went to a musical instrument store and bought her a piano as a gift. I excitedly put the purchase receipt in a box with a beautiful bow and gave it to her, expecting an effusive reaction of gratitude for her extremely loving and attentive husband.

When she opened that little box and saw its contents, she lovingly looked at me and said, "Oh, my dear, you are wonderful! But let me ask you a question: Is this a gift or a debt?" After counseling together about the surprise, we decided to cancel the purchase. We were living on a student budget, as is the case with many young newlyweds. This experience helped me recognize the importance of the principle of full partnership in a marital relationship and how its application could help my wife and me to be of one heart and one mind.[1]

The restored gospel of Jesus Christ proclaims the principle of full partnership between woman and man, both in mortal life and in the eternities. Although each possesses specific attributes and divinely appointed responsibilities, woman and man fill equally relevant and essential roles in God's plan of happiness for His children.[2] This was evident from the very beginning when the Lord declared "that it was not good that the man should be alone; wherefore [He would] make an help meet for him."[3]

In the Lord's plan, a "help meet" was a companion who would walk shoulder to shoulder with Adam in full partnership.[4] In fact, Eve was a heavenly blessing in Adam's life. Through her divine nature and spiritual attributes, she inspired Adam to work in partnership with her to achieve God's plan of happiness for all mankind.[5]

Let us consider two fundamental principles that strengthen the partnership between man and woman. The first principle is we are all alike unto God.[6] According to gospel doctrine, the difference between woman and man does not override the eternal promises that God has for His sons and daughters. One has no greater possibilities for celestial glory than the other in the eternities.[7] The Savior Himself invites all of us, God's children, "to come unto him and partake of his goodness; and he denieth none that come unto him."[8] Therefore, in this context, we are all considered equal before Him.

When spouses understand and incorporate this principle, they do not position themselves as president or vice president of their family. There is no superiority or inferiority in the marriage relationship, and neither walks ahead of or behind the other. They walk side by side, as equals, the divine offspring of God. They become one in thought, desire, and purpose with our Heavenly Father and Jesus Christ,[9] leading and guiding the family unit together.

In an equal partnership, "love is not possession, but participation, . . . part of that co-creation which is our human calling."[10] "With true participation, husband and wife merge into the synergistic oneness of an 'everlasting dominion' that 'without compulsory means' will flow with spiritual life to them and their posterity 'forever and ever.'"[11]

The second relevant principle is the Golden Rule, taught by the Savior in the Sermon on the Mount: "And as ye would that men should do to you, do ye also to them likewise."[12] This principle indicates an attitude of mutuality, reciprocity, unity, and interdependence and is based on the second great commandment: "Thou shalt love thy neighbour as thyself."[13] It merges with other Christian attributes such as long-suffering, gentleness, meekness, and kindness.

To better understand the application of this principle, we can look at the sacred and eternal bond established by God between our first parents, Adam and Eve. They became one flesh,[14] creating a dimension of unity that allowed them to walk together with respect, gratitude, and love, forgetting about themselves and seeking each other's well-being on their journey to eternity.

Those same characteristics are what we strive for in a united marriage today. Through the temple sealing, a woman and a man enter the holy order of matrimony in the new and everlasting covenant. By way of this order of the priesthood, they are given eternal blessings and divine power to direct their family affairs as they live according to the covenants they have made. From that point on, they move forward interdependently and in full partnership with the Lord, especially in regard to each of their divinely appointed responsibilities of nurturing and presiding in their family.[15] Nurturing and presiding are interrelated and overlapping responsibilities, which means that mothers and fathers "are obligated to help one another as equal partners"[16] and share a balanced leadership in their home.

"To nurture means to nourish, teach, and support" family members, which is done by helping them to "learn gospel truths and develop faith in Heavenly Father and Jesus Christ" in an environment of love. To preside means to "help lead family members back to dwell in God's presence. This is done by serving and teaching with gentleness, meekness, and pure love." It also includes "leading family members in regular prayer, gospel study, and other aspects of worship. Parents work in unity," following the example of Jesus Christ, "to fulfill these [two great] responsibilities."[17]

It is important to observe that the government in the family follows the patriarchal pattern, differing in some respects from priesthood leadership in the Church.[18] The patriarchal pattern entails that wives and husbands are accountable directly to God for the fulfillment of their sacred responsibilities in the family. It calls for a full partnership—a willing compliance with every principle of righteousness and accountability—and provides opportunities for development within an environment of love and mutual helpfulness.[19] These special responsibilities do not imply hierarchy and absolutely exclude any kind of abuse or improper use of authority.

The experience of Adam and Eve, after they left the Garden of Eden, beautifully illustrates the concept of interdependence between a mother and father in nurturing and presiding over their family. As taught in the book of Moses, they worked together to till the earth by the sweat of their brow in order to provide for the physical well-being of their family;[20] they brought children into the world;[21] they called on the name of the Lord together and heard His voice "from the way toward the Garden of Eden";[22] they accepted the commandments the Lord gave them and strove together to obey them.[23] They then "made [these] things known unto their sons and their daughters"[24] and "ceased not to call upon God" together according to their needs.[25]

My dear brothers and sisters, nurturing and presiding are opportunities, not exclusive limitations. One person may have a responsibility for something but may not be the only person doing it. When loving parents well understand these two major responsibilities, they will strive together to protect and care for the physical and emotional well-being of their children. They also help them face the spiritual dangers of our day by nurturing them with the good word of the Lord as revealed to His prophets.

Although husband and wife support each other in their divinely appointed responsibilities, "disability, death, or other circumstances may necessitate individual adaptation."[26] Sometimes one spouse or the other will have the responsibility of acting in both roles simultaneously, whether temporarily or permanently.

I recently met a sister and a brother who each live in this condition. As single parents, each of them, within their family sphere and in partnership with the Lord, has decided to devote their lives to the spiritual and temporal care of their children. They have not lost sight of their temple covenants made with the Lord and His eternal promises despite their divorces. Both have sought the Lord's help in all things as they continually strive to endure their challenges and walk in the covenant path. They trust that the Lord will take care of their needs, not only in this life but throughout eternity. Both have nurtured their children by teaching them with gentleness, meekness, and pure love, even while experiencing difficult circumstances in life. From what I know, these two single parents do not blame God for their misfortunes. Instead, they look forward with a perfect brightness of hope and confidence to the blessings the Lord has in store for them.[27]

Brothers and sisters, the Savior set the perfect example of unity and harmony of purpose and doctrine with our Father in Heaven. He prayed in behalf of His disciples, saying, "That they all may be one; as thou, Father, art in me, and I in thee, that they also may be one in us: . . . that they may be one, even as we are one."[28]

I testify to you that as we—women and men—work together in a true and equal partnership, we will enjoy the unity taught by the Savior as we fulfill the divine responsibilities in our marriage relationships. I promise you, in the name of Christ, that hearts will be "knit together in unity and in love one towards another,"[29] we will find more joy in our journey to eternal life, and our capacity to serve one another and with one another will multiply significantly.[30] I bear witness to these truths in the holy name of the Savior Jesus Christ, amen.

Notes

1. See Moses 7:18.
2. See "The Family: A Proclamation to the World," ChurchofJesusChrist.org.
3. Moses 3:18; see also Genesis 2:18.
4. "The Lord intended that the wife be a helpmeet for man (*meet* means equal)—that is, a companion equal and necessary in full partnership" (*Teachings of Presidents of the Church: Howard W. Hunter* [2015], 224).
5. See Moses 3:18–24; 4:12; 5:10–12.
6. See Romans 2:11; 1 Nephi 17:35; 2 Nephi 26:33.
7. See Mosiah 2:41.
8. 2 Nephi 26:33.
9. See Guide to the Scriptures, "Unity," scriptures.ChurchofJesusChrist.org.
10. Madeleine L'Engle, *The Irrational Season* (1977), 48.
11. Bruce C. Hafen and Marie K. Hafen, "Crossing Thresholds and Becoming Equal Partners," *Ensign*, Aug. 2007, 28; *Liahona*, Aug. 2007, 30; see also Doctrine and Covenants 121:45–46.
12. Luke 6:31; see also Matthew 7:12.
13. Mark 12:31.
14. See Genesis 2:23–24.
15. See "The Family: A Proclamation to the World," ChurchofJesusChrist.org.
16. "The Family: A Proclamation to the World," ChurchofJesusChrist.org.
17. See *General Handbook: Serving in The Church of Jesus Christ of Latter-day Saints*, 2.1.3, ChurchofJesusChrist.org.
18. See Doctrine and Covenants 107:21–26; see also *General Handbook*, 4.2.4.
19. See Dallin H. Oaks, "Priesthood Authority in the Family and the Church," *Ensign* or *Liahona*, Nov. 2005, 24–27; Ezra Taft Benson, "What I Hope You Will Teach Your Children about the Temple," *Ensign*, Aug. 1985, 6–10; *Tambuli*, Apr./May 1986, 1–6.
20. See Moses 5:1.
21. See Moses 5:2.
22. Moses 5:4.
23. See Moses 5:5.
24. Moses 5:12.
25. Moses 5:16.
26. "The Family: A Proclamation to the World," ChurchofJesusChrist.org.
27. See 2 Nephi 31:20.
28. John 17:21–22.
29. Mosiah 18:21.
30. See Henry B. Eyring, "Our Hearts Knit as One," *Ensign* or *Liahona*, Nov. 2008, 68–71.

AND THEY SOUGHT TO SEE JESUS WHO HE WAS

ELDER JAMES W. McCONKIE III
Of the Seventy

Brothers, sisters, and friends, in 2013 my wife, Laurel, and I were called to serve as mission leaders in the Czech/Slovak Mission. Our four children served with us.[1] We were blessed as a family with brilliant missionaries and by the remarkable Czech and Slovak Saints. We love them.

As our family entered the mission field, something Elder Joseph B. Wirthlin taught went with us. In a talk titled "The Great Commandment," Elder Wirthlin asked, "Do you love the Lord?" His counsel to those of us who would answer yes was simple and profound: "Spend time with Him. Meditate on His words. Take His yoke upon you. Seek to understand and obey."[2] Elder Wirthlin then promised transformative blessings to those willing to give time and place to Jesus Christ.[3]

We took Elder Wirthlin's counsel and promise to heart. Together with our missionaries, we spent extended time with Jesus, studying Matthew, Mark, Luke, and John from the New Testament and 3 Nephi from the Book of Mormon. At the end of every missionary meeting, we found ourselves back in what we referred to as the "Five Gospels,"[4] reading, discussing, considering, and learning about Jesus.

For me, for Laurel, and for our missionaries, spending time with Jesus in the scriptures changed everything. We gained a deeper appreciation for who He was and what was important to Him. Together we considered how He taught, what He taught, the ways He showed love, what He did to bless and serve, His miracles, how He responded to betrayal, what He did with difficult human emotions, His titles and names, how He listened, how He resolved conflict, the world He lived in, His parables, how He encouraged unity and kindness, His capacity to forgive and to heal, His sermons, His prayers, His atoning sacrifice, His Resurrection, His gospel.

We often felt like the "[short] of stature" Zacchaeus running to climb a sycamore tree as Jesus passed through Jericho because, as Luke described it, we "sought to see Jesus who he was."[5] It was not Jesus as we wanted or wished Him to be, but rather Jesus as He really was and is.[6] Just as Elder Wirthlin had promised, we learned in a very real way that "the gospel of Jesus Christ is a gospel of transformation. It takes us as men and women of the earth and refines us into men and women for the eternities."[7]

Those were special days. We came to believe that "with God nothing shall be impossible."[8] Sacred afternoons in Prague, Bratislava, or Brno, experiencing the power and reality of Jesus, continue to resonate in all of our lives.

We often studied Mark 2:1–12. The story there is compelling. I want to read part of it directly from Mark and then share it as I have come to understand it after comprehensive study and discussion with our missionaries and others.[9]

"And again [Jesus] entered into Capernaum after some days; and it was noised that he was in the house.

"And straightway many were gathered together, insomuch that there was no room to receive them, no, not so much as about the door: and he preached the word unto them.

"And they come unto him, bringing one sick of the palsy, which was borne of four.

"And when they could not come nigh unto him for the press, they uncovered the roof where he was: and when they had broken it up, they let down the bed wherein the sick of the palsy lay.

"When Jesus saw their faith, he said unto the sick of the palsy, Son, thy sins be forgiven thee."

After an exchange with some in the crowd,[10] Jesus looks at the man sick of palsy and heals him physically, saying:

"I say unto thee, Arise, and take up thy bed, and go thy way into thine house.

"And immediately he arose, took up the bed, and went forth before them all; insomuch that they were all amazed, and glorified God, saying, We never saw it on this fashion."[11]

63

Now the story as I have come to understand it: Early in His ministry, Jesus returned to Capernaum, a small fishing village located on the north shore of the Sea of Galilee.[12] He had recently performed a series of miracles by healing the sick and casting out evil spirits.[13] Anxious to hear and experience the man called Jesus, the villagers gathered at the home where He was rumored to be staying.[14] As they did, Jesus began to teach.[15]

Homes at that time in Capernaum were flat-roofed, single-story dwellings, grouped together.[16] The roof and walls were a mixture of stone, timber, clay, and thatch, accessed by a set of simple steps on the side of the home.[17] The crowd grew quickly at the house, filled the room where Jesus was teaching, and spread out into the street.[18]

The story focuses on a man "sick of the palsy" and his four friends.[19] Palsy is a form of paralysis, often accompanied by weakness and tremors.[20] I imagine one of the four saying to the others, "Jesus is in our village. We all know about the miracles He has performed and those He has healed. If we can just get our friend to Jesus, perhaps he too can be made whole."

So they each take a corner of their friend's mat or bed and begin carrying him through the crooked, narrow, unpaved streets of Capernaum.[21] Muscles aching, they turn the last corner only to find that the crowd or, as the scripture calls it, the "press" of people gathered to listen is so great that getting to Jesus is impossible.[22] With love and faith, the four do not give up. Rather, they scramble up the steps onto the flat roof, carefully lift their friend and his bed up with them, break open the roof over the room where Jesus is teaching, and let their friend down.[23]

Consider that in the middle of what must have been a serious teaching moment, Jesus hears a scratching noise, looks up, and sees a growing hole in the ceiling as dust and thatch fall into the room. A paralyzed man on a bed is then lowered to the floor. Remarkably, Jesus discerns that this is not an interruption but rather something that matters. He looks at the man on the bed, publicly forgives his sins, and physically heals him.[24]

With that telling of Mark 2 in mind, several important truths become clear about Jesus as the Christ. First, when we try to help someone we love come unto Christ, we can do so with confidence that He has the capacity to lift the burden of sin and to forgive. Second, when we bring physical, emotional, or other illnesses to Christ, we can do so knowing He has the power to heal and comfort. Third, when we make effort like the four to bring others to Christ, we can do so with certainty that He sees our true intentions and will appropriately honor them.

Remember, Jesus's teaching was disrupted by the appearance of a hole in the roof. Rather than chastise or dismiss the four who made the hole for interrupting, the scripture tells us that "Jesus *saw* their faith."[25] Those who witnessed the miracle then "marvelled, and glorified God, which had given such power [to] men."[26]

Brothers and sisters, let me close with two additional observations. Whether as missionaries, ministers, Relief Society presidents, bishops, teachers, parents, siblings, or friends, we are all engaged as Latter-day Saint disciples in the work of bringing others to Christ. Thus, the qualities exhibited by the four friends are worth considering and emulating.[27] They are bold, adaptive, resilient, creative, versatile, hopeful, determined, faithful, optimistic, humble, and enduring.

Additionally, the four emphasize the spiritual importance of community and fellowship.[28] In order to bring their friend to Christ, each of the four must carry their corner. If one lets go, things get more difficult. If two give up, the task effectively becomes impossible. Each of us has a role to play in the kingdom of God.[29] As we fill that role and do our part, we carry our corner. Whether in Argentina or Vietnam, Accra or Brisbane, a branch or a ward, a family or a missionary companionship, we each have a corner to carry. As we do, and if we will, the Lord blesses us all. As He saw *their* faith, so will He see *ours* and bless us as a people.

At different times I have carried the corner of a bed, and at other times I have been the one carried. Part of the power of this remarkable story of Jesus is that it reminds us just how much we need each other, as brothers and sisters, in order to come unto Christ and be transformed.

These are a few of the things I have learned from spending time with Jesus in Mark 2.

"May God grant that we may be able to [carry our corner], that we may not shirk, that we may not fear, but that we may be strong in our faith, and determined in our work, to accomplish the purposes of the Lord."[30]

I witness that Jesus lives, that He knows us, and that He has the power to heal, to transform, and to forgive. In the name of Jesus Christ, amen.

Notes

1. Evie, Wilson, Hyrum, and George.
2. Joseph B. Wirthlin, "The Great Commandment," *Ensign* or *Liahona*, Nov. 2007, 30.
3. The blessings identified by Elder Wirthlin include an increased capacity for love, a willingness to be obedient and responsive to God's commandments, a desire to serve others, and a disposition to do good continually.
4. "The Gospels . . . are a fourfold presentation under the names of four different evangelists or Gospel writers of the life and teaching of Jesus, and of his suffering, death and resurrection" (Anders Bergquist, "Bible," in John Bowden, ed., *Encyclopedia of Christianity* [2005], 141). The Bible Dictionary adds that "the word *gospel* means 'good news.' The good news is that Jesus Christ has made a perfect atonement for mankind that will redeem all mankind. . . . The records of His mortal life and the events pertaining to His ministry are called the Gospels" (Bible Dictionary, "Gospels"). 3 Nephi, recorded by Nephi, the grandson of Helaman, contains a record of the appearance and teaching of the resurrected Jesus Christ in the Americas just after His Crucifixion and therefore may also be referred to as a "Gospel." The Gospels are particularly compelling because they record events and circumstances in which Jesus Himself actively teaches and participates. They are a critical starting point for understanding Jesus as the Christ, our relationship to Him, and His gospel.
5. See Luke 19:1–4; see also Jacob 4:13 (explaining that the Spirit "speaketh of things as they really are, and of things as they really will be") and Doctrine and Covenants 93:24 (defining truth as "knowledge of things as they are, and as they were, and as they are to come").
6. President J. Reuben Clark similarly encouraged the study of "the life of the Savior as an actual personality." He invited others to be in the scriptural accounts of Jesus Christ's life, to try and "go along with the Savior, live with him, let him be an actual man, half divine, of course, but nevertheless moving as a man moved in those days." He furthermore promised that such an effort "will give you such a view of him, such an intimacy with him as I think you can get in no other way. . . . Learn what he did, what he thought, what he taught. Do as he did. Live as he lived, so far as we can. He was the perfect man" (*Behold the Lamb of God* [1962], 8, 11). For insight regarding the value and reasons for studying Jesus in the context of history, see N. T. Wright and Michael F. Bird, *The New Testament in Its World* (2019), 172–87.
7. Joseph B. Wirthlin, "The Great Commandment," 30.
8. Luke 1:37.
9. In addition to regular and extended discussion of Mark 2:1–12 with the missionaries of the Czech/Slovak Mission, I am also grateful for lessons learned considering this text with the young men and women of the Salt Lake Highland Stake missionary preparation class and the leaders and members of the Salt Lake Pioneer YSA Stake.
10. See Mark 2:6–10.

11. Mark 2:11–12.
12. See Bruce M. Metzger and Michael D. Coogan, eds., *The Oxford Companion to the Bible* (1993), 104; James Martin, *Jesus: A Pilgrimage* (2014), 183–84.
13. See Mark 1:21–45.
14. See Mark 2:1–2.
15. See Mark 2:2.
16. See Metzger and Coogan, *The Oxford Companion to the Bible*, 104; William Barclay, *The Gospel of Mark* (2001), 53.
17. See Barclay, *The Gospel of Mark*, 53; see also Martin, *Jesus: A Pilgrimage*, 184.
18. See Mark 2:2, 4; see also Barclay, *The Gospel of Mark*, 52–53. Barclay explains that "life in Palestine was very public. In the morning the door of the house was opened and anyone who wished might come out and in. The door was never shut unless someone deliberately wished for privacy; an open door meant an open invitation for all to come in. In the humbler [homes] such as [the one identified in Mark 2] must have been, there was no entrance hall; the door opened directly . . . to the street. So, in no time, a crowd had filled the house to capacity and jammed the pavement round the door; and they were all eagerly listening to what Jesus had to say."
19. Mark 2:3.
20. See *Medical Dictionary of Health Terms*, "palsy," health.harvard.edu.
21. See Martin, *Jesus: A Pilgrimage*, 184.
22. Mark 2:4.
23. See Mark 2:4; see also Julie M. Smith, *The Gospel according to Mark* (2018), 155–71.
24. See Mark 2:5–12.
25. Mark 2:5; emphasis added.
26. Matthew 9:8; see also Mark 2:12; Luke 5:26.
27. Doctrine and Covenants 62:3 explains that the Lord's servants are "blessed, for the testimony which ye have borne is recorded in heaven . . . and your sins are forgiven you."
28. See M. Russell Ballard, "Hope in Christ," *Liahona*, May 2021, 55–56. President Ballard notes that a "sense of belonging" is important to both physical and spiritual health, and he observes that "every member in our quorums, organizations, wards, and stakes has God-given gifts and talents that can help build up His kingdom now." See also David F. Holland, *Moroni: A Brief Theological Introduction* (2020), 61–65. Holland discusses Moroni 6 and the ways in which participation and fellowship in a faith community help facilitate the kind of personal spiritual experience that binds us more closely to heaven.
29. See Dieter F. Uchtdorf, "Lift Where You Stand," *Ensign* or *Liahona*, Nov. 2008, 56. Elder Uchtdorf explains that "none of us can or should move the Lord's work alone. But if we all stand close together in the place the Lord has appointed and lift where we stand, nothing can keep this divine work from moving upward and forward." See also Chi Hong (Sam) Wong, "Rescue in Unity," *Ensign* or *Liahona*, Nov. 2014, 15. Elder Wong references Mark 2:1–5 and teaches that "in order to assist the Savior, we have to work together in unity and in harmony. Everyone, every position, and every calling is important."
30. Oscar W. McConkie, in Conference Report, Oct. 1952, 57.

BUILDING A LIFE RESISTANT TO THE ADVERSARY

ELDER JORGE F. ZEBALLOS

Of the Seventy

Over the years from this beautiful pulpit at the Conference Center, we have received magnificent counsel, inspiration, instruction, and revelation. On occasion, speakers have used comparisons associated with their areas of knowledge and experience to illustrate clearly and powerfully a principle of the gospel of Jesus Christ.

In this way, for example, we have learned about airplanes and flights in which a tiny initial deviation can lead us to a place far from our original destination.[1] Also in this way, we have learned from a comparison of the function of our physical heart with the powerful change of heart required to respond to the Lord's invitation to follow Him.[2]

This time, I would like to humbly add a comparison inspired from an area in the field of my professional preparation. I am referring to the world of civil engineering. From the beginning of my university studies, I dreamed of the day when I would complete the requirements to be qualified to take the class that would teach me how to design buildings and other structures that could then be considered "anti-seismic."

The day finally arrived for my first class on this subject. The first words from the professor were the following: "You are surely anxious to begin this course and learn how to design anti-seismic structures," to which many of us eagerly nodded our heads. Then the professor said, "I am sorry to tell you that this is not possible, for I cannot teach you how to design a building that is against, that is 'anti-' or that is opposed to, an earthquake. This makes no sense," he said, "because earthquakes will occur anyway, whether we like it or not."

Then he added, "What I can teach you is how to design structures that are seismic-resistant, structures that can resist the forces coming from an earthquake, so that the structure remains standing without suffering any serious damage and can then continue offering the service for which it had been conceived."

The engineer makes the calculations that indicate the dimensions, qualities, and characteristics of the foundations, columns, beams, concrete slabs, and other structural elements being designed. These results are translated into plans and technical specifications, which must be strictly followed by the builder in order for the work to materialize and thus fulfill the purpose for which it was designed and is being built.

Although more than 40 years have passed since that first class in seismic-resistant engineering, I perfectly remember the moment when I began to acquire a deeper, more complete understanding of the vital importance that this concept would be present in the structures that I would design in my future professional life. Not only that, but even more important—that it would be permanently present in the edification of my own life and in those over whom I might exercise a positive influence.

How blessed we are to count on a knowledge of the plan of salvation created by our Heavenly Father, to have the restored gospel of Jesus Christ, and to rely on the inspired direction of living prophets! All the former constitute the divinely designed "plans" and the "technical specifications" that teach us clearly how to construct happy lives—lives that are resistant to sin, resistant to temptation, resistant to attacks from Satan, who is desperately seeking to frustrate our eternal destiny to be together with our Heavenly Father and with our beloved families.

The Savior Himself, at the beginning of His ministry, "was left to be tempted of the devil."[3] But Jesus emerged successful from that great trial. How did having an attitude of anti-Satan or anti-temptation serve Him? What made Jesus emerge triumphant from these most difficult moments was His spiritual preparation, which permitted Him to be in a condition to resist the temptations of the adversary.

What were some of the factors that helped the Savior to be prepared for that crucial moment?

First, He had fasted for 40 days and 40 nights, a fast that must have been accompanied by constant prayer. So, although He was physically weak, His spirit was very strong. Even though, fortunately, we are not asked to fast for such a duration—rather for only 24 hours and once a month—fasting brings us spiritual strength and prepares us to be resistant to the trials of this life.

In the second place, in the account of the temptations to which the Savior was submitted, we see that He always answered Satan having scriptures in His mind, quoting them, and applying them at the right moment.

When Satan tempted Him to convert stones into bread so that He could satisfy His hunger from His long fast, the Lord said to him, "It is written, Man shall not live by bread alone, but by every word that proceedeth out of the mouth of God."[4] Then, when the Lord was on the pinnacle of the temple, the devil tried to tempt Him to demonstrate His power, to which the Lord answered with authority, "It is written again, Thou shalt not tempt the Lord thy God."[5] And to Satan's third attempt, the Lord responded, "It is written, Thou shalt worship the Lord thy God, and him only shalt thou serve."[6]

The event of an earthquake leaves its mark even on structures that were correctly designed and built—such consequences as perhaps some cracks, fallen furniture or ceilings, and broken windows. But this well-designed and well-built edifice will fulfill its purpose of protecting its occupants, and with some repairs, it will recuperate its original condition.

In similar fashion, the buffetings of the adversary can also cause "cracks," or some partial damage in our lives, in spite of our efforts to build our lives according to the perfect divine design. These "cracks" can manifest themselves through feelings of sadness or remorse for having committed some errors and for not having done everything perfectly, or for feeling that we are not as good as we want to be.

But what is truly relevant is that for having followed the divinely designed plans and specifications, that is, the gospel of Jesus Christ, we are still standing. The structure of our lives has not been demolished because of the adversary's efforts or for difficult situations that we have had to face; rather, we are ready to move forward.

The joy promised in the scriptures as the purpose of our existence[7] should not be understood to mean that we will have no difficulties or sorrows, that we will have no "cracks" as consequences of temptations, of adversity, or from the actual trials of our earth life.

This joy has to do with Nephi's perspective on life when he said, "Having seen many afflictions in the course of my days, nevertheless, having been highly favored of the Lord in all my days."[8] All his days! Even the days that Nephi suffered during the incomprehension and rejection of his own brothers, even when they tied him up on the ship, even the day that his father, Lehi, passed away, even when Laman and Lemuel became mortal enemies of his people. Even in those difficult days, Nephi felt highly favored of the Lord.

We can have the tranquility of knowing that the Lord will never permit us to be tempted beyond what we can resist. Alma invites us to "watch and pray continually, that [we] may not be tempted above that which [we] can bear, and thus be led by the Holy Spirit, becoming humble, meek, submissive, patient, full of love and all long-suffering."[9]

The same can be applied to the trials of life. Ammon reminds us of the words of the Lord: "Go . . . and bear with patience thine afflictions, and I will give unto you success."[10]

The Lord always provides us with help when we face adversity, temptation, incomprehension, infirmities, and even death. He has said, "And now, verily I say unto you, and what I say unto one I say unto all, be of good cheer, little children; for I am in your midst, and I have not forsaken you."[11] He will never abandon us!

I pray that we may continue to build our lives following the plans and technical specifications of the divine design authored by our Father and achieved through our Savior, Jesus Christ. Thus, because of the grace that reaches us through the Atonement of our Savior, we will be successful in constructing a life resistant to sin, resistant to temptation, and strengthened to endure the sad, difficult times in our lives. And furthermore, we will be in a condition to access all the blessings promised through the love of our Father and our Savior. In the name of Jesus Christ, amen.

Notes

1. See Dieter F. Uchtdorf, "A Matter of a Few Degrees," *Ensign* or *Liahona*, May 2008, 57–60.
2. See Dale G. Renlund, "Preserving the Heart's Mighty Change," *Ensign* or *Liahona*, Nov. 2009, 97–99.
3. Joseph Smith Translation, Matthew 4:2 (in Matthew 4:2, footnote *c*).
4. Matthew 4:4.
5. Matthew 4:7.
6. Matthew 4:10.
7. See 2 Nephi 2:25.
8. 1 Nephi 1:1.
9. Alma 13:28.
10. Alma 26:27.
11. Doctrine and Covenants 61:36.

THE DOCTRINE OF BELONGING

ELDER D. TODD CHRISTOFFERSON
Of the Quorum of the Twelve Apostles

I would like to speak about what I call the doctrine of belonging in The Church of Jesus Christ of Latter-day Saints. This doctrine has three parts: (1) the role of belonging in gathering the Lord's covenant people, (2) the importance of service and sacrifice in belonging, and (3) the centrality of Jesus Christ to belonging.

The Church of Jesus Christ of Latter-day Saints in its early beginnings was made up largely of white North American and northern European Saints with a relative handful of Native Americans, African Americans, and Pacific Islanders. Now, eight years away from the 200th anniversary of its founding, the Church has greatly increased in numbers and diversity in North America and even more so in the rest of the world.

As the long-prophesied latter-day gathering of the Lord's covenant people gains momentum, the Church will truly be composed of members from every nation, kindred, tongue, and people.[1] This is not a calculated or forced diversity but a naturally occurring phenomenon that we would expect, recognizing that the gospel net gathers from every nation and every people.

How blessed we are to see the day that Zion is being established simultaneously on every continent and in our own neighborhoods. As the Prophet Joseph Smith said, the people of God in every age have looked forward with joyful anticipation to this day, and "we are the favored people that God has made choice of to bring about the Latter-day glory."[2]

Having been given this privilege, we cannot permit any racism, tribal prejudice, or other divisions to exist in the latter-day Church of Christ. The Lord commands us, "Be one; and if ye are not one ye are not mine."[3] We should be diligent in rooting prejudice and discrimination out of the Church, out of our homes, and, most of all, out of our hearts. As our Church population grows ever more diverse, our welcome must grow ever more spontaneous and warm. We need one another.[4]

In his First Epistle to the Corinthians, Paul declares that all who are baptized into the Church are one in the body of Christ:

"For as the body is one, and hath many members, and all the members of that one body, being many, are one body: so also is Christ.

"For by one Spirit are we all baptized into one body, whether we be Jews or Gentiles, whether we be bond or free; and have been all made to drink into one Spirit. . . .

"That there should be no schism in the body; but that the members should have the same care one for another.

"And whether one member suffer, all the members suffer with it; or one member be honoured, all the members rejoice with it."[5]

A sense of belonging is important to our physical, mental, and spiritual well-being. Yet it is quite possible that at times each of us might feel that we don't fit in. In discouraging moments, we may feel that we will never measure up to the Lord's high standards or the expectations of others.[6] We may unwittingly impose expectations on others—or even ourselves—that are not the Lord's expectations. We may communicate in subtle ways that the worth of a soul is based on certain achievements or callings, but these are not the measure of our standing in the Lord's eyes. "The Lord looketh on the heart."[7] He cares about our desires and longings and what we are becoming.[8]

Sister Jodi King wrote of her own experience of past years:

"I never felt like I didn't belong at church until my husband, Cameron, and I began struggling with infertility. The children and families who had typically brought me joy to see at church now started causing me grief and pain.

"I felt barren without a child in my arms or a diaper bag in hand. . . .

"The hardest Sunday was our first one in a new ward. Because we didn't have kids, we were asked if we were newlyweds and when we planned on starting a family. I had gotten pretty good at answering these questions without letting them affect me—I knew they weren't meant to be hurtful.

"However, on this particular Sunday, answering those questions was especially hard. We had just found out, after being hopeful, that we were—yet again—not pregnant.

"I walked into sacrament meeting feeling downtrodden, and answering those typical 'get to know you' questions was hard for me. . . .

"But it was Sunday School that truly broke my heart. The lesson—intended to be about the divine role of mothers—quickly shifted gears and became a vent[ing] session. My heart sank and tears silently flowed down my cheeks as I heard women complain about a blessing I would give anything for.

"I bolted out of church. At first, I didn't want to go back. I didn't want to experience that feeling of isolation again. But that night, after talking with my husband, we knew we would keep attending church not only because the Lord has asked us to but also because we both knew that the joy that comes from renewing covenants and feeling the Spirit at church surpasses the sadness I felt that day. . . .

"In the Church, there are widowed, divorced, and single members; those with family members who have fallen away from the gospel; people with chronic illnesses or financial struggles; members who experience same-sex attraction; members working to overcome addictions or doubts; recent converts; new move-ins; empty-nesters; and the list goes on and on. . . .

"The Savior invites us to come unto Him—no matter our circumstances. We come to church to renew our covenants, to increase our faith, to find peace, and to do as He did perfectly in His life—minister to others who feel like they don't belong."[9]

Paul explained that the Church and its officers are given by God "for the perfecting of the saints, for the work of the ministry, for the edifying of the body of Christ:

"Till we all come in the unity of the faith, and of the knowledge of the Son of God, unto a perfect man, unto the measure of the stature of the fulness of Christ."[10]

It is a sad irony, then, when someone, feeling he or she doesn't meet the ideal in all aspects of life, concludes that he doesn't or she doesn't belong in the very organization designed by God to help us progress toward the ideal.

Let us leave judgment in the Lord's hands and those He has commissioned and be content to love and treat each other the best we can. Let us ask Him to show us the way, day by day, to "bring in . . . the poor, and the maimed, and the halt, and the blind"[11]—that is, everyone—to the great feast of the Lord.

A second facet of the doctrine of belonging has to do with our own contributions. Although we rarely think about it, much of our belonging comes from our service and the sacrifices we make for others and for the Lord. Excessive focus on our personal needs or our own comfort can frustrate that sense of belonging.

We strive to follow the Savior's doctrine:

"Whosoever will be great among you, shall be your *minister*. . . .

"For even the Son of man came not to be ministered unto, but to minister, and to give his life a ransom for many."[12]

Belonging comes not as we wait for it but as we reach out to help one another.

Today, unfortunately, consecrating oneself to a cause or sacrificing anything for anyone else is becoming countercultural. In a piece for *Deseret Magazine* last year, author Rod Dreher recounted a conversation with a young mother in Budapest:

"I am on a Budapest tram with a . . . friend in her early 30s— let's call her Kristina—while we are on the way to interview an older [Christian] woman who, with her late husband, withstood persecution by the communist state. As we bump along the city's streets, Kristina talks about how hard it is to be honest with friends her age about the struggles she faces as a wife and mother of young children.

"Kristina's difficulties are completely ordinary for a young woman learning how to be a mom and a wife—yet the prevailing attitude among her generation is that life's difficulties are a threat to one's well-being and should be refused. Do she and her husband argue at times? Then she should leave him, they say. Are her children annoying her? Then she should send them to day care.

"Kristina worries that her friends don't grasp that trials, and even suffering, are a normal part of life—and maybe even part of a good life, if that suffering teaches us how to be patient, kind and loving. . . .

". . . University of Notre Dame sociologist of religion Christian Smith found in his study of adults [ages] 18 to 23 that most of them believe society is nothing more than 'a collection of autonomous individuals out to enjoy life.'"[13]

By this philosophy, anything that one finds difficult "is a form of oppression."[14]

By contrast, our pioneer forebears derived a deep sense of belonging, unity, and hope in Christ by the sacrifices they made to serve missions, build temples, abandon comfortable homes under duress and begin again, and in a multitude of other ways consecrate themselves and their means to the cause of Zion. They were willing to sacrifice even their lives if necessary. And we are all the beneficiaries of their endurance. The same is true for many today who may lose family and friends, forfeit employment opportunities, or otherwise suffer discrimination or intolerance as a consequence of being baptized. Their reward, however, is a powerful sense of belonging among the covenant people. Any sacrifice we make in the Lord's cause helps to confirm our place with Him who gave His life a ransom for many.

The final and most important element of the doctrine of belonging is the central role of Jesus Christ. We don't join the Church for fellowship alone, important as that is. We join for redemption through the love and grace of Jesus Christ. We join to secure the ordinances of salvation and exaltation for ourselves and those we love on both sides of the veil. We join to participate in a great project to establish Zion in preparation for the Lord's return.

The Church is the custodian of the covenants of salvation and exaltation that God offers us through the ordinances of the holy priesthood.[15] It is by keeping these covenants that we obtain the highest and deepest sense of belonging. President Russell M. Nelson recently wrote:

"Once you and I have made a covenant with God, our relationship with Him becomes much closer than before our covenant. Now we are bound together. Because of our covenant with God, He will never tire in His efforts to help us, and we will never exhaust His merciful patience with us. Each of us has a special place in God's heart. . . .

". . . Jesus Christ is the guarantor of those covenants (see Hebrews 7:22; 8:6)."[16]

If we will remember this, the Lord's high hopes for us will inspire, not discourage, us.

We can feel joy as we pursue, individually and communally, "the measure of the stature of the fulness of Christ."[17] Despite disappointments and setbacks along the way, it is a grand quest. We lift and encourage each other in pursuing the upward path, knowing that no matter tribulation and no matter delays in promised blessings, we can "be of good cheer; [for Christ has] overcome the world,"[18] and we are with Him. Being one with the Father, Son, and Holy Spirit is without doubt the ultimate in belonging.[19]

Thus, the doctrine of belonging comes down to this—each one of us can affirm: Jesus Christ died for me; He thought me worthy of His blood. He loves me and can make all the difference in my life. As I repent, His grace will transform me. I am one with Him in the gospel covenant; I belong in His Church and kingdom; and I belong in His cause to bring redemption to all of God's children.

I testify you do belong, in the name of Jesus Christ, amen.

Notes

1. See Revelation 5:9; see also 1 Nephi 19:17; Mosiah 15:28; Doctrine and Covenants 10:51; 77:8, 11.
2. *Teachings of Presidents of the Church: Joseph Smith* (2007), 186.
3. Doctrine and Covenants 38:27.
4. One perceptive observer noted:

"Religion that is merely a private affair has been, until our time, unknown in the annals of mankind—and for good reason. Such religion quickly diminishes into an indoor pleasure, a kind of hobby of one or more individuals, like reading a book or watching television. So it is not astonishing that the search for spirituality has become so fashionable. It is what individuals, liberated from religion, desperately seek as a substitute.

"Spirituality is indeed an integral part of all religions—but a minor part, and it cannot be a substitute for the whole. Religion is not some kind of psychic exercise that occasionally offers a transcendental experience. It either shapes one's life—all of one's life—or it vanishes, leaving behind anxious, empty souls that no psychotherapy can reach. And for religion to shape one's life, it needs to be public and communal; it needs to be connected to the dead and the unborn" (Irving Kristol, "The Welfare State's Spiritual Crisis," *Wall Street Journal*, Feb. 3, 1997, A14).

5. 1 Corinthians 12:12–13, 25–26.

6. See Russell M. Nelson, "Perfection Pending," *Ensign*, Nov. 1995, 86–88; Jeffrey R. Holland, "Be Ye Therefore Perfect—Eventually," *Ensign* or *Liahona*, Nov. 2017, 40–42.

7. 1 Samuel 16:7.

8. As expressed by Elder Jeffrey R. Holland, "'Come as you are,' a loving Father says to each of us, but He adds, 'Don't plan to stay as you are.' We smile and remember that God is determined to make of us more than we thought we could be" ("Songs Sung and Unsung," *Ensign* or *Liahona*, May 2017, 51).

9. Jodi King, "Belonging in the Church through the Lens of Infertility," *Ensign*, Mar. 2020, 72, 74–75; *Liahona*, Mar. 2020, 46, 48–49.

10. Ephesians 4:12–13.

11. Luke 14:21.

12. Mark 10:43, 45; emphasis added.

13. Rod Dreher, "A Christian Survival Guide for a Secular Age," *Deseret Magazine*, Apr. 2021, 68.

14. Dreher, "A Christian Survival Guide for a Secular Age," 68.

15. See Doctrine and Covenants 84:19–22.

16. Russell M. Nelson, "The Everlasting Covenant," *Liahona*, Oct. 2022, 6, 10.

17. Ephesians 4:13.

18. John 16:33.

19. See John 17:20–23. "And now, I would commend you to seek this Jesus of whom the prophets and apostles have written, that the grace of God the Father, and also the Lord Jesus Christ, and the Holy Ghost, which beareth record of them, may be and abide in you forever" (Ether 12:41).

SATURDAY EVENING SESSION

———

OCTOBER 1, 2022

OUR EARTHLY STEWARDSHIP

BISHOP GÉRALD CAUSSÉ
Presiding Bishop

While visiting our native country of France, my wife and I recently had the pleasure of taking a few of our grandchildren to explore a magnificent garden situated in the little town of Giverny. We enjoyed wandering along its paths to admire the beautiful flower beds, the elegant water lilies, and the light playing on the ponds.

This amazing place is the result of the creative passion of one man: the great painter Claude Monet, who, for 40 years, tenderly shaped and cultivated his garden to make it his painting workspace. Monet immersed himself in nature's splendor; then, with his paintbrush, he conveyed the impressions he felt with strokes of color and light. Over the years, he created an extraordinary collection of hundreds of paintings, directly inspired by his garden.

Brothers and sisters, our interactions with the beauties of nature around us can produce some of the most inspiring and delightful experiences in life. The emotions we feel kindle within us a deep sense of gratitude for our Heavenly Father and His Son, Jesus Christ, who created this magnificent earth—with its mountains and streams, plants and animals—and our first parents, Adam and Eve.[1]

The work of creation is not an end in itself. It is an integral part of God's plan for His children. Its purpose is to provide the setting in which men and women may be tested, exercise their agency, find joy, and learn and progress so that they may one day return to the presence of their Creator and inherit eternal life.

These wonderful creations were prepared entirely for our benefit and are living proof of the love the Creator has for His children. The Lord declared, "Yea, all things which come of the earth . . . are made for the benefit and the use of man, both to please the eye and to gladden the heart."[2]

However, the divine gift of the Creation does not come without duties and responsibilities. These duties are best described by the concept of *stewardship*. In gospel terms, the word *stewardship* designates a sacred spiritual or temporal responsibility to take care of something that belongs to God for which we are accountable.[3]

As taught in the holy scriptures, our earthly stewardship includes the following principles:

First principle: The entire earth, including all life thereon, belongs to God.

The Creator has entrusted the earth's resources and all forms of life to our care, but He retains full ownership. He said, "I, the Lord, stretched out the heavens, and built the earth, my very handiwork; and all things therein are mine."[4] All that is on the earth belongs to God, including our families, our physical bodies, and even our very lives.[5]

Second principle: As stewards of God's creations, we have a duty to honor and care for them.

As God's children, we have received the charge to be stewards, caretakers, and guardians of His divine creations. The Lord said that He made "every man accountable, as a steward over earthly blessings, which I have made and prepared for my creatures."[6]

Our Heavenly Father allows us to use earthly resources according to our own free will. Yet our agency should not be interpreted as license to use or consume the riches of this world without wisdom or restraint. The Lord gave this admonition: "And it pleaseth God that he hath given all these things unto man; for unto this end were they made to be used, with judgment, not to excess, neither by extortion."[7]

President Russell M. Nelson once remarked: "As beneficiaries of the divine Creation, what shall we do? We should care for the earth, be wise stewards over it, and preserve it for future generations."[8]

Beyond being simply a scientific or political necessity, the care of the earth and of our natural environment is a sacred responsibility entrusted to us by God, which should fill us with a deep sense of duty and humility. It is also an integral component of our discipleship. How can we honor and love Heavenly Father and Jesus Christ without honoring and loving Their creations?

There are many things that we can do—collectively and individually—to be good stewards. Considering our individual circumstances, each of us can use the bountiful resources of the earth more reverently and prudently. We can support community efforts to care for the earth. We can adopt personal lifestyles and behaviors that respect God's creations and make our own living spaces tidier, more beautiful, and more inspirational.[9]

Our stewardship over God's creations also includes, at its pinnacle, a sacred duty to love, respect, and care for all human beings with whom we share the earth. They are sons and daughters of God, our sisters and our brothers, and their eternal happiness is the very purpose of the work of creation.

The author Antoine de Saint-Exupéry recounted the following: One day, while traveling on a train, he found himself sitting amidst a group of refugees. Deeply moved by the hopelessness he saw in the face of a young child, he exclaimed: "When by mutation a new rose is born in a garden, all the gardeners rejoice. They isolate the rose, tend it, foster it. But there is no gardener for men."[10]

My brothers and sisters, should we not be the gardeners for our fellow men and women? Are we not our brother's keeper? Jesus commanded us to love our neighbor as ourselves.[11] From His mouth, the word *neighbor* does not merely mean geographic proximity; it implies a proximity of the heart. It encompasses all the inhabitants of this planet—whether they live near us or in a faraway country, regardless of their origins, personal backgrounds, or circumstances.

As disciples of Christ, we have a solemn duty to work tirelessly for peace and harmony among all nations of the earth. We must do our very best to protect and bring solace and relief to the weak, the needy, and all those who suffer or who are oppressed. Above all, the greatest gift of love we can offer our fellow men is to share with them the joy of the gospel and invite them to come unto their Savior through sacred covenants and ordinances.

Third principle: We are invited to participate in the work of creation.

The divine process of creation is not yet complete. Every day, God's creations continue to grow, expand, and multiply. A most wonderful thing is that our Heavenly Father extends to us an invitation to participate in His creative work.

We participate in the work of creation whenever we cultivate the earth or add our own constructions to this world—as long as we show respect for God's creations. Our contributions may be expressed through the creation of works of art, architecture, music, literature, and culture, which embellish our planet, quicken our senses, and brighten our lives. We also contribute through scientific and medical discoveries that preserve the earth and life upon it. President Thomas S. Monson summarized this concept with these beautiful words: "God left the world unfinished for man to work his skill upon . . . that man might know the joys and glories of creation."[12]

In Jesus's parable of the talents, when the master returned from his journey, he praised and rewarded the two servants who grew and magnified their talents. In contrast, he called the servant who hid his unique talent in the earth "unprofitable," and he took away even that which he had received.[13]

Similarly, our role as stewards of earthly creations is not solely about conserving or preserving them. The Lord expects us to work diligently, as moved upon by His Holy Spirit, to grow, enhance, and improve upon the resources He has entrusted to us—not for our benefit only but to bless others.

Among all of man's achievements, none can equal the experience of becoming *cocreators* with God in giving life or in helping a child learn, grow, and thrive—whether it be as parents, teachers, or leaders, or in any other role. There is no stewardship more sacred, more fulfilling, and also more demanding than that of partnering with our Creator in providing physical bodies for His spirit children and then helping them reach their divine potential.

The responsibility of cocreation serves as a constant reminder that life and each person's body are sacred, that they belong to none other than God, and that He has made us guardians to respect, protect, and care for them. The commandments of God, which govern the powers of procreation and the establishment of eternal families, guide us in this holy stewardship, which is so crucial to His plan.

My brothers and sisters, we should recognize that all is spiritual to the Lord—including the most temporal aspects of our lives. I testify that great spiritual blessings are promised to those who love and care for the earth and their fellow men and women. As you stay faithful in this sacred stewardship and honor your eternal covenants, you will grow in the knowledge of God and of His Son, Jesus Christ, and you will feel Their love and Their influence more abundantly in your life. All this will prepare you to dwell with Them and receive additional creative power[14] in the life to come.

At the end of this mortal existence, the Master will ask us to give an account for our sacred stewardship, including how we have cared for His creations. I pray that we will then hear His loving words whispered to our hearts: "Well done, thou good and faithful servant: thou hast been faithful over a few things, I will make thee ruler over many things: enter thou into the joy of thy lord."[15] In the name of Jesus Christ, amen.

Notes

1. The earth and all things upon it (with the exception of Adam and Eve) were created by Jesus Christ under the direction of the Father; Adam and Eve, our first parents, were created by God the Father (see John 1:1–3; Moses 2:1, 26–27).
2. Doctrine and Covenants 59:18.
3. See Spencer W. Kimball, "Welfare Services: The Gospel in Action," *Ensign*, Nov. 1977, 76–79.
4. Doctrine and Covenants 104:14.
5. See Spencer W. Kimball, "Welfare Services," 76–79.
6. Doctrine and Covenants 104:13.
7. Doctrine and Covenants 59:20.
8. Russell M. Nelson, "The Creation," *Ensign*, May 2000, 86; *Liahona*, July 2000, 104.
9. See Gospel Topics, "Environmental Stewardship and Conservation," topics.ChurchofJesusChrist .org.
10. Antoine de Saint-Exupéry, *Terre des Hommes* (1939), 214; see also *Wind, Sand and Stars* (1939) in *Airman's Odyssey* (1984), 206.
12. See Mark 12:31.
13. Thomas S. Monson, "In Quest of the Abundant Life," *Ensign*, Mar. 1988, 2; "In Search of an Abundant Life," *Tambuli*, August 1988, 3.
14. See Matthew 25:14–30.
15. See David A. Bednar and Susan K. Bednar, "Moral Purity" (Brigham Young University–Idaho devotional, Jan. 7, 2003), byui.edu.
16. Matthew 25:21.

WHOLEHEARTED

SISTER MICHELLE D. CRAIG

First Counselor in the Young Women General Presidency

Sometimes, it helps to know what to expect.

Near the end of His ministry, Jesus told His Apostles that hard times would come. But He also said, "See that ye be not troubled."[1] Yes, He would leave, but He would not leave them alone.[2] He would send His Spirit to help them remember, stand fast, and find peace. The Savior fulfills His promise to be with us, His disciples, but we must continually look to Him to help us recognize and enjoy His presence.

Christ's disciples have always encountered hard times.

A dear friend of mine sent me an old article from the *Nebraska Advertiser*, a Midwestern United States newspaper, dated July 9, 1857. It read: "This morning early a company of Mormons passed through on their journey to Salt Lake. Women (not very delicate to be sure) dragging hand carts like beasts, one [woman] tumbled down in this black mud which caused a slight halt in the procession, little children trudged along in their [strange] foreign dress looking as determined as their mothers."[3]

I've thought a lot about this mud-drenched woman. Why was she pulling alone? Was she a single mother? What gave her the inner strength, the grit, the perseverance to make such a wrenching journey through mud, pulling all her possessions in a handcart to an unknown desert home—at times being mocked by observers?[4]

President Joseph F. Smith spoke of the inner strength of these pioneer women, saying: "Could you turn one of these women away from their convictions in the Church of Jesus Christ of Latter-day Saints? Could you darken their minds as to the mission of the Prophet Joseph Smith? Could you blind them with reference to the divine mission of Jesus Christ, the Son of God? No, never in the world could you do it. Why? Because they knew it. God revealed it to them, and they understood it, and no power on earth could turn them from what they knew to be that truth."[5]

Brothers and sisters, to be such men and women is the call of our day—disciples who dig deep to find the strength to keep pulling when called to walk through the wilderness, disciples with convictions that have been revealed to us by God, followers of Jesus who are joyful and wholehearted in our own personal journey of discipleship. As disciples of Jesus Christ, we believe and can grow in three important truths.

First, We Can Keep Our Covenants, Even When It Is Not Easy

When your faith, your family, or your future are challenged—when you wonder why life is so hard when you are doing your best to live the gospel—remember that the Lord told us to expect troubles. Troubles are part of the plan and do not mean you've been abandoned; they are part of what it means to be His.[6] He was, after all, "a man of sorrows, and acquainted with grief."[7]

I am learning that Heavenly Father is more interested in my *growth* as a disciple of Jesus Christ than He is with my *comfort*. I may not always want it to be that way—but it is!

Living in convenience does not bring power. The power we need to withstand the heat of our day is the *Lord's* power, and His power flows through our covenants with Him.[8] To lean in with our faith when facing strong headwinds—to sincerely strive each day to *do* what we covenanted with the Savior we would *do*, even and especially when we are tired, worried, and wrestling with troubling questions and issues—is to gradually receive His light, His strength, His love, His Spirit, His peace.

The point of walking the covenant path is to approach the Savior. *He* is the point, not our perfect progress. It is not a race, and we must not compare our journey to others'. Even when we stumble, He is there.

Second, We Can Act in Faith

As disciples of Jesus Christ, we understand that faith in Him requires action—especially in hard times.[9]

Many years ago, my parents decided to recarpet the house. The night before the new carpet arrived, my mom asked my brothers to remove furniture and rip out bedroom carpets so the new carpet could be installed. My then seven-year-old sister, Emily, was already asleep. So, while she slept, they quietly removed all the furniture from her room, except the bed, and then tore out the carpet. Well, like older brothers sometimes do, they decided to pull a prank. They removed the rest of her belongings from the closet and off the walls, leaving the room bare. Then they wrote a note and tacked it to the wall: "Dear Emily, we moved. We'll write in a few days and tell you where we are. Love, your family."

The next morning when Emily did not come for breakfast, my brothers went to find her—there she was, sad and alone behind a closed door. Emily reflected on this experience later: "I was crushed. But what would have happened if I had just opened the door? What would I have heard? What would I have smelled? I would have known I was not alone. I would have known I really was loved. The thought never even crossed my mind to do something about my situation. I just gave up and stayed in my closet crying. And yet if I had simply opened the door."[10]

My sister made an assumption based on what she saw, but it wasn't a reflection of the way things actually were. Isn't it interesting that we, like Emily, can become so weighed down in sadness or hurt or discouragement or worry or loneliness or anger or frustration that it doesn't even occur to us to simply do something, to open the door, to act with faith in Jesus Christ?

The scriptures are filled with examples of men and women, disciples of Christ, who, when facing the impossible, simply acted—who got up in faith and walked.[11]

To lepers who sought healing, Christ said: "Go shew yourselves unto the priests. And it came to pass, that, *as they went*, they were cleansed."[12]

They went to show themselves to the priests as if they had already been healed, and in the process of acting, they were.

I also want to say if the thought of taking action amid your pain feels impossible, please let your action be to reach out for help—to a friend, a family member, a Church leader, a professional. This can be a first step to hope.

Third, We Can Be Wholehearted and Joyful in Our Devotion[13]

When hard times come, I try to remember that I chose to follow Christ before I came to earth and that challenges to my faith, my health, and my endurance are all part of the reason I'm here. And I certainly should never think that today's trial calls into question God's love for me or let it turn my faith in Him into doubt. Trials do not mean that the plan is failing; they are part of the plan meant to help me seek God. I become more like Him when I endure patiently, and hopefully, like Him, when in agony, I pray more earnestly.[14]

Jesus Christ was the perfect example of loving our Father with all His heart—of doing His will, regardless of the cost.[15] I want to follow His example by doing the same.

I am inspired by the wholehearted, whole-souled discipleship of the widow who threw her two mites into the temple treasury. She gave her all.[16]

Jesus Christ recognized the abundance of her all where others saw only her lack. The same is true with each of us. He doesn't see our lack as failure but rather as an opportunity to exercise faith and to grow.

Conclusion

My fellow disciples of Jesus Christ, with all my heart, I choose to stand with the Lord. I choose to stand with His chosen servants—President Russell M. Nelson and his fellow Apostles—for they speak for Him and are the stewards of the ordinances and covenants that tie me to the Savior.

When I stumble, I will keep getting up, relying on the grace and enabling power of Jesus Christ. I will stay in my covenant with Him and work through my questions by study of God's word, by faith, and with the help of the Holy Ghost, whose guidance I trust. I will seek His Spirit every day by doing the small and simple things.

This is my path of discipleship.

And until the day that the everyday wounds of mortality are healed, I will wait upon the Lord and trust Him—His timing, His wisdom, His plan.[17]

Arm in arm with you, I want to stand with Him forever. Wholehearted. Knowing that when we love Jesus Christ with all our hearts, He gives us all in return.[18] In the name of Jesus Christ, amen.

Notes

1. Matthew 24:6.
2. See Matthew 24:13; Joseph Smith—Matthew 1:11; see also Matthew 28:19–20; John 14:18.
3. Netty Penwood, "Leaves from My Iowa Log Book," *Nebraska Advertiser*, July 9, 1857, 1, newspapers.com/clip/60679566/pioneers-trek-to-the-salt-lake-valley/.
4. See 1 Nephi 8:27.
5. *Teachings of Presidents of the Church: Joseph F. Smith* (1998), 189.
6. See John 16:33; Revelation 7:13–17; Abraham 3:25.
7. Isaiah 53:3.
8. See M. Russell Ballard, "Like a Flame Unquenchable," *Ensign*, May 1999, 86; *Liahona*, July 1999, 102.
9. See Bible Dictionary, "Faith."
10. Personal correspondence.
11. See Joshua 3:5, 13, 15–17; 2 Kings 5:14; Matthew 14:29; Mark 2:3–5; Luke 8:43–44; John 2:3–5; Acts 11:12; 1 Nephi 4:6–7; 16:23; 3 Nephi 27:21; Ether 2:16; 3; Moses 6:32, 42.
12. Luke 17:14; emphasis added; see also verses 11–13.
13. "When the focus of our lives is on . . . Jesus Christ and His gospel, we can feel joy regardless of what is happening—or not happening—in our lives" (President Russell M. Nelson, "Joy and Spiritual Survival," *Ensign* or *Liahona*, Nov. 2016, 82).
14. See Luke 22:44.
15. See Matthew 26:39, 42, 44.
16. See Mark 12:41–44.
17. See Isaiah 40:31.
18. See Romans 8:14–18, 28, 38–39.

ARE YOU STILL WILLING?

ELDER KEVIN W. PEARSON
Of the Seventy

One Sunday, while I was preparing to partake of the sacrament after several weeks of stake conference assignments, an interesting and powerful thought passed through my mind.

As the priest began offering the blessing on the bread, words I had heard so many times before pressed forcefully upon my mind and heart. "And *witness unto thee*, O God, the Eternal Father, that *they are willing* to *take upon them the name of thy Son*, and *always remember him* and *keep his commandments* which he has given them; that they *may always have his Spirit to be with them*."[1] How many times have we witnessed unto God that we are willing?

As I pondered the significance of those sacred words, the word *willing* impressed me as never before. A flood of sweet and sacred experiences filled my mind and heart with love and gratitude for the atoning sacrifice of the Savior and His crucial role in the Father's plan of redemption for my family and me. Then I heard and felt the penetrating words of the prayer on the water: "That they may witness unto thee . . . that they do always remember him."[2] I understood clearly in that moment that keeping my covenants must be more than good intentions.

Partaking of the sacrament is not a passive religious ritual implying our mere consent. It is a powerful reminder of the reality of the Savior's infinite Atonement and the need to always remember Him and keep His commandments. Willingness to focus on the Savior is so crucial it is the central message of the two most quoted scriptures in the Church: the sacrament prayers. Understanding the truth of what Heavenly Father so willingly offers each of us through His Only Begotten Son should evoke our utmost efforts to always be willing in return.

Is our own spiritual foundation built solidly on Jesus Christ?

If our spiritual foundation is shallow or superficial, we might be inclined to base our willingness on a social cost-benefit analysis or a personal inconvenience index. And if we embrace the narrative that the Church consists primarily of outdated or politically incorrect social policies, unrealistic personal restrictions, and time commitments, then our conclusions about willingness will be flawed. We should not expect the principle of willingness to trend positively with social media influencers or TikTok enthusiasts. The precepts of men rarely align with divine truth.

The Church is a gathering place for imperfect individuals who love God and who are willing to follow the Lord Jesus Christ. That willingness is rooted in the reality that Jesus is the Christ, the Son of the living God. This divine truth can be known only by the power of the Holy Ghost. Therefore, our willingness is directly proportionate to the amount of time we commit to be in holy places where the influence of the Holy Ghost is present.

We would do well to spend more time in meaningful conversation discussing our concerns with a loving Father in Heaven and less time seeking the opinions of other voices. We could also choose to change our daily news feed to the words of Christ in the holy scriptures and to prophetic words of His living prophets.

The importance we place on our Sabbath day observance, paying an honest tithe, holding a current temple recommend, attending the temple, and honoring our sacred temple covenants are all powerful indicators of our willingness and evidence of our commitment. Are we willing to put forth more than a superficial effort into strengthening our faith in Christ?

Heavenly Father loves us perfectly, but that love comes with great expectations. He expects us to willingly place the Savior at the very center of our lives. The Savior is our perfect example of willingness to submit to the Father in all things. He is "the way, the truth, and the life."[3] He willingly atoned for our sins. He willingly eases our burdens, calms our fears, gives us strength, and brings peace and understanding to our hearts in times of distress and grief.

Yet faith in Jesus Christ is a choice. "If [we] can no more than desire to believe"[4] in His words, we have a starting point to begin or to reset our journey of faith. His words, if planted in our hearts like a seed and nourished with great care, will take root and our faith will grow into assurance and become a principle of action and power. The Book of Mormon is our most powerful resource for growing and restoring our faith. Willingness is the catalyst of faith.

Mortality, by divine design, is not easy and at times can be overwhelming. However, "[we] are, that [we] might have joy"![5] Focusing on the Savior and our covenants brings lasting joy! The purpose of mortality is to prove our willingness. "*The great task of life* [and the cost of discipleship] is to learn the will of the Lord and then to do it."[6] True discipleship leads to a fulness of joy. Are we willing to pay the price of discipleship?

The covenant path is not a simple checklist; it is a process of spiritual growth and deepening commitment to the Lord Jesus Christ. The central purpose of every commandment, principle, covenant, and ordinance is to build faith and trust in Christ. Our determination to center our lives on Christ, therefore, must be consistent—not conditional, situational, or superficial. We cannot afford to take vacation days or personal time off from our willingness to "stand as witnesses of God at all times and in all things, and in all places."[7] Discipleship is not cheap, because the companionship of the Holy Ghost is priceless.

Surely the Lord was thinking of our day as He taught the parable of the ten virgins. Of the five who were wise, He said they "have taken the Holy Spirit for their guide, and have not been deceived,"[8] while the lamps of the foolish "are gone out" for lack of oil.[9] Perhaps the words of Nephi best describe these once-faithful members of the Church: "And others he will pacify, and lull them away into carnal security, that they will say: All is well in Zion."[10]

Carnal security is seeking for and trusting in worldly things instead of Christ—in other words, looking through a secular lens instead of a spiritual lens. The Holy Ghost gives us the capacity to see "things as they really are, and . . . as they really will be."[11] Only "by the power of the Holy Ghost [can we] know the truth of all things"[12] and be not deceived. We place Christ at the center of our lives and pledge our willingness to obey His commandments not because we are blind but because we can see.[13]

What about the foolish virgins? Why were they unwilling to carry a vessel of spiritual oil? Did they simply procrastinate? They were perhaps too casual because it was inconvenient or seemed unnecessary. Whatever the reason, they were deceived about the crucial role of Christ. This is Satan's fundamental deception and why their lamps of testimony eventually went out for lack of spiritual oil. This parable is a metaphor for our time. Many leave the Savior and their covenants long before they leave His Church.

We live in unprecedented times long foretold by ancient prophets, a day when Satan rages "in the hearts of the children of men, and stir[s] them up to anger against that which is good."[14] Far too many of us live in a virtual world awash in entertainment and messaging hostile to divine identity and belief in Christ.

The most powerful spiritual influence in the life of a child is the righteous example of loving parents and grandparents who faithfully keep their own sacred covenants. Intentional parents teach their children faith in the Lord Jesus Christ so that they too "may know to what source they may look for a remission of their sins."[15] Casual and inconsistent covenant keeping leads to spiritual casualty. The spiritual damage is often greatest on our children and grandchildren. Parents and grandparents, are we still willing?

President Russell M. Nelson has warned that "in coming days, it will not be possible to survive spiritually without the guiding, directing, comforting, and constant influence of the Holy Ghost."[16] This is a clear and unmistakable warning to trim our lamps and increase our spiritual oil reserves. Are we still willing to follow the living prophets? What is the level of spiritual oil in your lamp? What changes in your personal life would enable you to have the influence of the Holy Ghost more constantly?

Today, as in the times of Jesus, there will be those who will turn back, unwilling to accept the price of discipleship. As harsh and hateful criticism is increasingly leveled at the Savior's Church and those who follow Him, our discipleship will require a greater willingness to straighten and strengthen our spiritual spines and heed them not.[17]

If our spiritual foundation is built solidly on Jesus Christ, we will not fall and we need not fear.

"Behold, the Lord requireth the heart and a willing mind; and the willing and obedient shall eat the good of the land of Zion in these last days."[18]

May we always be willing. In the sacred name of the Lord Jesus Christ, amen.

Notes

1. Doctrine and Covenants 20:77; emphasis added.
2. Doctrine and Covenants 20:79.
3. John 14:6.
4. Alma 32:27.
5. 2 Nephi 2:25.
6. Ezra Taft Benson, "The Great Commandment—Love the Lord," *Ensign*, May 1988, 4.
7. Mosiah 18:9.
8. Doctrine and Covenants 45:57.
9. Matthew 25:8.
10. 2 Nephi 28:21.
11. Jacob 4:13.
12. Moroni 10:5.
13. See Boyd K. Packer, "Agency and Control," *Ensign*, May 1983, 66.
14. 2 Nephi 28:20.
15. 2 Nephi 25:26.
16. Russell M. Nelson, "Revelation for the Church, Revelation for Our Lives," *Ensign* or *Liahona*, May 2018, 93.
17. See 1 Nephi 8:26–27, 33.
18. Doctrine and Covenants 64:34.

COURAGE TO PROCLAIM THE TRUTH

ELDER DENELSON SILVA

Of the Seventy

In 1982, I was finishing my associate's degree in topography at a technical school.

At the end of the year, a classmate invited me to have a conversation. I remember that we left the other members of the class and went to an area beside a sports court. When we got there, he spoke to me about his religious convictions, and not only did he show me a book, but he gave me the book. Honestly, I do not remember all the words that he said, but I remember that moment very well and the way I felt when he said, "I want to bear my testimony to you that this book is true and that the gospel of Jesus Christ has been restored."

After our conversation, I went home, turned a few pages in the book, and placed it on a shelf. Because we were at the end of the year and it was the last year of my topography degree, I did not really pay much attention to the book or to my classmate who had shared it with me. The name of the book you can already guess. Yes, it was the Book of Mormon.

Five months later, the missionaries came into my house; they were leaving just as I was coming home from work. I invited them back in. We sat down in the little patio in front of my house, and they taught me.

In my search for the truth, I asked them which church was true and how I could find it. The missionaries taught me that I could obtain that answer for myself. With great expectation and desire, I accepted their challenge to read several chapters from the Book of Mormon. I prayed with a sincere heart and with real intent (see Moroni 10:4–5). The answer to my question was clear, and several days later—more precisely on May 1, 1983—I was baptized and confirmed a member of The Church of Jesus Christ of Latter-day Saints.

Today, when I think about the sequence of events that occurred, I see clearly how important the courage of my classmate was when he bore his testimony about the restored truth and presented me with tangible proof of the Restoration of the gospel of Jesus Christ, even the Book of Mormon. That simple act, but of profound significance to me, created a connection between me and the missionaries when I met them.

The truth had been presented to me, and after my baptism, I became a disciple of Jesus Christ. During the following years, and with the help of very special people such as leaders, teachers, and friends, and also through my own personal study, I learned that when I decided to be a disciple of Jesus Christ, I had accepted the task of not only defending the truth but also proclaiming it.

When we agree to believe in the truth and to follow it, and when we make an effort to become true disciples of Jesus Christ, we do not receive a certificate with a guarantee that we will not make mistakes, that we will not be tempted to walk away from the truth, that we will not be criticized, or even that we will not experience afflictions. But the knowledge of the truth teaches that when we enter the strait and narrow path that will take us back to the presence of Heavenly Father, there will always be a way to escape these problems (see 1 Corinthians 10:13); there will always be the possibility of doubting our doubts before doubting our faith (see Dieter F. Uchtdorf, "Come, Join with Us," *Ensign* or *Liahona*, Nov. 2013, 21); and finally, we have a guarantee that we will never be alone when we go through afflictions, for God visits His people in the midst of their afflictions (see Mosiah 24:14).

Once we learn the truth, the Lord gives us the opportunity to do what He would do if He were here today. Truly, He showed us by His teachings what we must do: "And ye shall go forth in the power of my Spirit, preaching my gospel, two by two, in my name, lifting up your voices as with the sound of a trump, declaring my word like unto angels of God" (Doctrine and Covenants 42:6). The opportunity for missionary service in our youth is unique!

Please, young men, do not postpone your preparation to serve the Lord as missionaries. As you face situations that may make the decision to serve a mission a difficult one—such as interrupting your studies for a time, saying goodbye to your girlfriend without any guarantee that you will ever date her again, or even having to walk away from a job—remember the Savior's example. During His ministry, He likewise faced difficulty, including criticism, persecution, and ultimately the bitter cup of His atoning sacrifice. Yet in all circumstances He sought to do the will of His Father and give glory to Him. (See John 5:30; 6:38–39; 3 Nephi 11:11; Doctrine and Covenants 19:18–19.)

Young women, you are very welcome, if you so desire, to work in the vineyard of the Lord, and as you prepare yourselves to serve as full-time missionaries, you will not be exempt from the same challenges.

To all who decide to serve Him, I promise you that the 24 or 18 months of service will pass in the mission field just as they would pass if you stayed home, but the opportunities that await the worthy young men and young women of this Church in the mission field are unique. The privilege of representing the Savior Jesus Christ and His Church cannot be ignored. Participating in countless prayers, developing and bearing your testimony several times during the day, studying the scriptures for many hours, and meeting people whom you would never meet if you had stayed home are indescribable experiences. The same level of experience is reserved for the youth whom the Lord calls to serve on service missions. You are very welcome and necessary. Please do not minimize the importance of a service mission, for service missions also provide indescribable experiences. "The worth of souls is great in the sight of God" (Doctrine and Covenants 18:10), including the worth of your soul.

Upon returning from your service, perhaps your girlfriend or boyfriend is no longer waiting for you, but you will have learned very well how to make effective contacts. Your academic studies will make more sense with the glimpses you have had about preparing more adequately for the workplace, and finally, you will have the full certainty of having courageously proclaimed the gospel of peace, testifying about the restored truth.

For those of you who are married and at different stages of your life, you are very necessary in the work of the Lord. Prepare yourselves. Live healthy lives, seeking for temporal and spiritual self-reliance, because the opportunities to do what the Lord would do for His children are not limited to one age-group. The most delightful experiences my wife and I have had in recent years have come while serving alongside special couples, serving in special places, and serving very special people.

The experience I had at the end of my topography degree taught me that we always defend the truth when we proclaim it and that defending the truth is a proactive thing. The defense of the truth should never be done in an aggressive manner but rather with genuine interest to love, share, and invite the people we are testifying to about the truth, thinking only about the temporal and spiritual welfare of the children of a loving Heavenly Father (see Mosiah 2:41).

In general conference of October 2021, President Russell M. Nelson, our beloved prophet, taught that contrary to what some think, there really is what we call right and wrong. There really does exist an absolute truth—an eternal truth. (See "Pure Truth, Pure Doctrine, and Pure Revelation," *Liahona*, Nov. 2021, 6.)

The holy scriptures teach us, "Truth is knowledge of things as they are, and as they were, and as they are to come" (Doctrine and Covenants 93:24).

The knowledge of the truth does not make us better than other people, but it teaches us what we must do to return to God's presence.

As you proceed firmly in Christ and with courage not only to proclaim the truth but to live the truth, you will find comfort and peace during the turbulence that you shall encounter in these days.

The challenges of life can knock us down, but know that when we exercise faith in Jesus Christ, "[our] afflictions shall be but a small moment" (Doctrine and Covenants 121:7) in the grand scope of eternity. Please do not create a deadline for the end of your difficulties and challenges. Trust in Heavenly Father and do not give up, for if we do give up, we will never know how the end of our journey would have been in the kingdom of God.

Hold on to the truth, learning from the sources of truth:

- The scriptures (see 2 Nephi 32:3).
- The words of the prophets (see Amos 3:7).
- The Holy Ghost (see John 16:13).

I bear my testimony of Jesus Christ and that this is His Church. We have a living prophet, and we will always feel free when we proclaim the truth with courage. In the name of Jesus Christ, amen.

DRAWING CLOSER TO THE SAVIOR

ELDER NEIL L. ANDERSEN
Of the Quorum of the Twelve Apostles

My dear brothers and sisters, this evening I speak to the humble and devoted followers of Jesus Christ. As I see the goodness of your lives and your faith in our Savior here in this country and in the nations across the world, I love you all the more.

Toward the end of His ministry, Jesus's disciples asked Him to tell them of "the sign of [His Second Coming], and of the end of the world."[1]

Jesus told them of the conditions that would precede His return and concluded by declaring, "When ye shall see all these things, [you will] know that [the time] is near."[2]

In the last general conference, I listened very closely to the words of President Henry B. Eyring: "Each of us," he said, "wherever we are, knows that we live in increasingly perilous times. . . . Anyone with eyes to see the signs of the times and ears to hear the words of prophets knows that is true."[3]

The Savior commended His valiant disciples: "Blessed are *your* eyes, for they see: and *your* ears, for they hear."[4] May this blessing be ours as we listen closely to the words of the Lord through His prophets and others in this conference.

Wheat and Tares

The Lord explained that in this final time prior to His return, the "wheat," whom He describes as "the children of the kingdom,"[5] would grow side by side with the "tares," or those who do not love God and do not keep His commandments. They would "both grow together,"[6] side by side.

This will be our world until the Savior returns, with much that is good and much that is evil on every side.[7]

You may at times not feel like a strong, mature strand of wheat. Be patient with yourself! The Lord said that the wheat would include tender blades springing up.[8] We are all His Latter-day Saints, and although not yet all we want to be, we are serious in our desire to be His true disciples.

Strengthen Our Faith in Jesus Christ

We realize that as evil increases in the world, our spiritual survival, and the spiritual survival of those we love, will require that we more fully nurture, fortify, and strengthen the roots of our faith in Jesus Christ. The Apostle Paul counseled us to be rooted,[9] grounded, and settled[10] in our love for the Savior and our determination to follow Him. Today and the days ahead require more focused and concentrated effort, guarding against diversions and carelessness.[11]

But even with the increasing worldly influences around us, we need not fear. The Lord will never desert His covenant people. There is a compensatory power of spiritual gifts and divine direction for the righteous.[12] This added blessing of spiritual power, however, does not settle upon us just because we are part of this generation. It comes as we strengthen our faith in the Lord Jesus Christ and keep His commandments, as we come to know Him and love Him. "This is life eternal," Jesus prayed, "that they might know thee the only true God, and Jesus Christ, whom thou hast sent."[13]

As we know very well, having faith in Jesus Christ and being a true disciple is more than a one-time decision—more than a one-time event. It is a sacred, ongoing process that grows and expands through the seasons of our lives, continuing until we kneel at His feet.

With the wheat growing amidst the tares in the world, how can we deepen and strengthen our commitment to the Savior in the days ahead?

Here are three thoughts:

Immerse Ourselves in the Life of Jesus

First, we can immerse ourselves more completely into Jesus's life, His teachings, His majesty, His power, and His atoning sacrifice. The Savior said, "Look unto me in every thought."[14] The Apostle John reminds us, "We love him, because he first loved us."[15] As we better experience His love, we love Him even more and, very naturally, better follow His example of loving and caring for those around us. With every righteous movement toward Him, we see Him more clearly.[16] We adore Him, and we try in our small ways to emulate Him.[17]

Make Covenants with the Lord

Next, as we better know and love the Savior, we desire even more to promise Him our allegiance and trust. We make covenants with Him. We begin with our promises at baptism, and we confirm these promises and others as we repent daily, ask for forgiveness, and eagerly anticipate receiving the sacrament each week. We pledge to "always remember him and keep his commandments."[18]

When we are ready, we embrace the ordinances and covenants of the temple. Feeling the influence of eternity in our sacred, quiet moments in the house of the Lord, we gladly make covenants with God and strengthen our resolve to keep them.

Making and keeping covenants allows the love of the Savior to sink more deeply into our heart. In this month's *Liahona*, President Russell M. Nelson said: "[Our] covenant[s] will lead us closer and closer to Him. . . . God will not abandon His relationship with those who have forged such a bond with Him."[19] And as President Nelson said so beautifully this morning, "With the dedication of each new temple, additional godly power comes into the world to strengthen us and counteracts the intensifying efforts of the adversary."[20]

Can we see why the Lord would direct His prophet to bring the holy temples closer to us and allow us to be in His house more often?

As we enter the temple, we are freed for a time from the worldly influences crowding against us as we learn of our purpose in life and the eternal gifts offered us through our Savior, Jesus Christ.

Safeguard the Gift of the Holy Ghost

Finally, my third thought: in this sacred quest, we treasure, protect, defend, and safeguard the gift of the Holy Ghost. Both President M. Russell Ballard earlier and Elder Kevin W. Pearson just moments ago spoke of President Nelson's prophetic warning that I will repeat again: "It will not be possible to survive spiritually without the guiding, directing, comforting, and constant influence of the Holy Ghost."[21] It is a gift beyond price. We do our very best to protect our daily experiences so the influence of the Holy Ghost remains with us. We are a light to the world, and when necessary, we willingly choose to be different from others. President Dallin H. Oaks recently asked young adults: "Do [you] 'dare to be different?' . . . [Especially] important . . . are the choices you are making in your personal life. . . . Are you going forward against the world's opposition?"[22]

Choose to Be Different from the World

In a recent social media post, I asked fellow disciples to share choices they had made that required them to be different from the world. I received hundreds of responses.[23] Here are just a few:

Amanda: I am a nurse working in the local jail. I try caring for inmates as Christ would.

Rachel: I am an opera singer, and it's often taken for granted that I will wear whatever costume I'm given, regardless of modesty. [Because I am endowed,] I told [the producers] that the costume would need to be [modest]. They were unhappy . . . but reluctantly made the alterations. I wouldn't trade the peace that comes from standing as a witness of Christ at all times.

Chriss: I'm an alcoholic (in recovery), temple-worthy, member of the Church. I'm not quiet about my experiences with addiction and gaining a testimony of the Atonement [of Jesus Christ].

Lauren: I was writing a skit with my classmates in high school. They wanted to have my quiet, reserved character have a sudden outburst of profanity. They kept pressuring me, but I refused and held my ground.

Adam: A lot of people do not believe me when I say I keep the law of chastity and choose to abstain from pornography. They don't understand the advantage of joy and peace of mind it gives me.

Ella: My father is a member of the LGBTQ community. I always try to keep other people's feelings in consideration while standing as a witness of Christ and being true to what I believe.

Andrade: I decided to continue to go to church when my family decided not to go anymore.

And finally, from Sherry: We were attending an event at the governor's mansion. They began handing out champagne for a "toast." I insisted on water, although the staff said it would be offensive. We toasted the governor, and I held my water glass high! The governor was not offended.

President Nelson said, "Yes, you are living in the world, but you have very different standards from the world to help you avoid the stain of the world."[24]

Anastasia, a young mother in Ukraine, was in the hospital having just given birth to a baby boy as the bombings began in Kyiv this past February. A nurse opened the hospital room door and said with an urgent voice, "Take your baby, wrap him in a blanket, and go into the hall—now!"

Later, Anastasia commented:

"I never imagined my first days of motherhood would be so difficult, . . . but . . . I am focusing on . . . the blessings and miracles I have seen. . . .

"Right now, . . . it might seem impossible to ever forgive those who have caused so much destruction and harm . . . , but as a disciple of Christ, I have faith that I will be able to [forgive]. . . .

"I don't know all that will happen in the future . . . but I know that keeping our covenants will allow the Spirit to be with us continually, . . . allowing us to feel joy and hope, . . . even during difficult times."[25]

The Promise of Eternal Life and Celestial Glory

My brothers and sisters, I have been blessed to abundantly receive the love of our beloved Savior, Jesus Christ. I know He lives and guides His holy work. I do not fully have the words to express my love for Him.

We are all "children of the covenant" stretching across the earth in nations and cultures on every continent, numbering in the millions, as we await the glorious return of our Lord and Savior. Shining as a light to those around us, we consciously shape our desires, thoughts, choices, and actions. Seeking with all our heart to know and love the Savior, we separate ourselves from the world through covenants with God, being distinct, uncommon, and special, as we honor Him and His teachings without isolating ourselves from others who believe differently.

It is a wondrous journey to be wheat among the tares, sometimes fraught with heartache but always calmed by the maturing and assuring settling of our faith. As you allow your love for the Savior and His love for you to sink deep into your heart, I promise you added confidence, peace, and joy in meeting the challenges of your life. And the Savior promises us: "I [will] gather together my people, according to the parable of the wheat and the tares, that the wheat may be secured in the garners to possess eternal life, and be crowned with celestial glory."[26] In the name of Jesus Christ, amen.

Notes

1. Matthew 24:3.
2. Matthew 24:33.
3. Henry B. Eyring, "Steady in the Storms," *Liahona*, May 2022, 27.
4. Matthew 13:16; emphasis added.
5. Matthew 13:38.
6. Matthew 13:30.
7. Elder Neal A. Maxwell said: "Church members will live in this wheat-and-tares situation until the Millennium. Some real tares even masquerade as wheat" ("Becometh as a Child," *Ensign*, May 1996, 68).
8. See Doctrine and Covenants 86:4, 6.
9. See Colossians 2:7.
10. See Colossians 1:23; see also Ephesians 3:17; Neal A. Maxwell, "Grounded, Rooted, Established, and Settled" (Brigham Young University devotional, Sept. 15, 1981), speeches.byu.edu.
11. In Matthew 13:22, Jesus cautioned His disciples to not allow the cares of the world and the deceitfulness of riches to "choke the word" and stop their spiritual progress. I like to tie the phrase "choke the word" to the first chapter of John, where John declares the word to be Jesus: "In the beginning was the Word, and the Word was with God. . . . All things were made by him; and without him was not any thing made that was made" (John 1:1, 3). Our faith in Jesus Christ, our determination to follow Him, our love for the Savior can be choked, or prevented from growing, as it is deprived of spiritual light and nourishment (see Alma 32:37–41).
12. See Neil L. Andersen, "A Compensatory Spiritual Power for the Righteous" (Brigham Young University devotional, Aug. 18, 2015), speeches.byu.edu.

13. John 17:3.

14. Doctrine and Covenants 6:36.

15. 1 John 4:19.

16. Elder David B. Haight said:

    "It is true that some have actually seen the Savior, but when one consults the dictionary, he learns that there are many other meanings of the word *see*, such as coming to know Him, discerning Him, recognizing Him and His work, perceiving His importance, or coming to understand Him.

    "Such heavenly enlightenment and blessings are available to each of us" ("Temples and Work Therein," *Ensign*, Nov. 1990, 61).

17. See Mosiah 5:13.

18. Doctrine and Covenants 20:77.

19. Russell M. Nelson, "The Everlasting Covenant," *Liahona*, Oct. 2022, 5.

20. Russell M. Nelson, "What Is True?," *Liahona*, Nov. 2022, 29.

21. Russell M. Nelson, "Revelation for the Church, Revelation for Our Lives," *Ensign* or *Liahona*, May 2018, 96.

22. Dallin H. Oaks, "Going Forward in the Second Century" (Brigham Young University devotional, Sept. 13, 2022), speeches.byu.edu. President Oaks credited the phrase "dare to be different" to a recent article in the *Deseret Magazine* by Elder Clark G. Gilbert, the Church Educational System Commissioner, on preserving religious identity in higher education (see "Dare to Be Different," *Deseret Magazine*, Sept. 2022, deseret.com).

23. If you would like to learn from others who commented on how they have been different from the world, you can read their comments on Facebook (see Neil L. Andersen, Facebook, Aug. 18, 2022, facebook.com/neill.andersen) or Instagram (see Neil L. Andersen, Instagram, Aug. 18, 2022, instagram.com/neillandersen).

24. Russell M. Nelson, "Hope of Israel" (worldwide youth devotional, June 3, 2018), HopeofIsrael .ChurchofJesusChrist.org.

25. Anastasia Kocheva, "Facing the Conflict in Ukraine, Healing the Conflict in My Heart," *YA Weekly*, May 2022.

26. Doctrine and Covenants 101:65.

SUNDAY MORNING SESSION

———

OCTOBER 2, 2022

LIFTED UP UPON THE CROSS

ELDER JEFFREY R. HOLLAND
Of the Quorum of the Twelve Apostles

Years ago, following a graduate school discussion on American religious history, a fellow student asked me, "Why have the Latter-day Saints not adopted the cross that other Christians use as a symbol of their faith?"

Inasmuch as such questions about the cross are often a question about our commitment to Christ, I immediately told him that The Church of Jesus Christ of Latter-day Saints considers the atoning sacrifice of Jesus Christ to be the central fact, the crucial foundation, the chief doctrine, and the ultimate expression of divine love in God's grand plan for the salvation of His children.[1] I explained that the saving grace inherent in that act was essential for and universally gifted to the entire human family from Adam and Eve to the end of the world.[2] I quoted the Prophet Joseph Smith, who said, "All . . . things which pertain to our religion are only appendages" to the Atonement of Jesus Christ.[3]

Then I read him what Nephi had written 600 years before Jesus's birth: "And . . . the angel spake unto me . . . , saying: Look! And I looked and beheld the Lamb of God, . . . [who] was lifted up upon the cross and slain for the sins of the world."[4]

With my "love, share, and invite" zeal now kicking into high gear, I kept reading! To the Nephites in the New World the resurrected Christ said, "My Father sent me that I might be lifted up upon the cross; . . . that I might draw all men unto me, . . . and for this cause have I been lifted up."[5]

I was about to quote the Apostle Paul when I noticed that my friend's eyes were starting to glaze over. A quick look at his wristwatch apparently reminded him that he needed to be somewhere—anywhere—and he dashed off to his fictitious appointment. Thus ended our conversation.

This morning, some 50 years later, I am determined to finish that explanation—even if every single, solitary one of you start looking at your wristwatches. As I attempt to explain why we generally do *not* use the iconography of the cross, I wish to make abundantly clear our deep respect and profound admiration for the faith-filled motives and devoted lives of those who do.

One reason we do not emphasize the cross as a symbol stems from our biblical roots. Because crucifixion was one of the Roman Empire's most agonizing forms of execution, many early followers of Jesus chose not to highlight that brutal instrument of suffering. The meaning of Christ's death was certainly central to their faith, but for some 300 years they typically sought to convey their gospel identity through other means.[6]

By the fourth and fifth centuries, a cross was being introduced as a symbol of generalized Christianity, but ours is not a "generalized Christianity." Being neither Catholic nor Protestant, we are, rather, a *restored* church, *the restored* New Testament Church. Thus, our origins and our authority go back *before* the time of councils, creeds, and iconography.[7] In this sense, the absence of a symbol that was late coming into common use is yet another evidence that The Church of Jesus Christ of Latter-day Saints is a restoration of true Christian beginnings.

Another reason for not using iconized crosses is our emphasis on the complete miracle of Christ's mission—His glorious Resurrection as well as His sacrificial suffering and death. In underscoring that relationship, I note two pieces of art[8] that serve as backdrops for the First Presidency and Quorum of the Twelve Apostles in their sacred weekly temple meetings each Thursday in Salt Lake City. These portrayals serve as constant reminders to us of the price that was paid and the victory that was won by Him whose servants we are.

A more public representation of Christ's two-part triumph is our use of this small Thorvaldsen image of the resurrected Christ emerging in glory from the tomb with the wounds of His Crucifixion still evident.[9]

Lastly, we remind ourselves that President Gordon B. Hinckley once taught, "The lives of our people must [be] . . . the symbol of our [faith]."[10] These considerations—especially the latter—bring me to what may be the most important of all scriptural references to the cross. It has nothing to do with pendants or jewelry, with steeples or signposts. It has to do, rather, with the rock-ribbed integrity and stiff moral backbone that Christians should bring to the call Jesus has given to every one of His disciples. In every land and age, He has said to us all, "If any man [or woman] will come after me, let him deny himself, and take up his cross, and follow me."[11]

This speaks of the crosses we bear rather than the ones we wear. To be a follower of Jesus Christ, one must sometimes carry a burden—your own or someone else's—and go where sacrifice is required and suffering is inevitable. A true Christian cannot follow the Master only in those matters with which he or she agrees. *No.* We follow Him everywhere, including, if necessary, into arenas filled with tears and trouble, where sometimes we may stand very much alone.

I know people, in and out of the Church, who are following Christ just that faithfully. I know children with severe physical disabilities, and I know the parents who care for them. I see all of them working sometimes to the point of total exhaustion, seeking strength, safety, and a few moments of joy that come no other way. I know many single adults who yearn for and deserve a loving companion, a wonderful marriage, and a home full of children of their own. No desire could be more righteous, but year after year such good fortune does not yet come. I know those who are fighting mental illness of many kinds, who plead for help as they pray and pine and claw for the promised land of emotional stability. I know those who live with debilitating poverty but, defying despair, ask only for the chance to make better lives for their loved ones and others in need around them. I know many who wrestle with wrenching matters of identity, gender, and sexuality. I weep for them, and I weep with them, knowing how significant the consequences of their decisions will be.

These are just a few of so many trying circumstances we may face in life, solemn reminders that there *is* a cost to discipleship. To Araunah, who attempted to give him free oxen and free wood for his burnt offering, King David said, "Nay; but I will surely buy it of thee at a price: . . . [for I] will [not] offer . . . unto the Lord my God . . . that which doth cost me nothing."[12] So too say we all.

As we take up our crosses and follow Him, it would be tragic indeed if the weight of our challenges did not make us more empathetic for and more attentive to the burdens being carried by others. It is one of the most powerful paradoxes of the Crucifixion that the arms of the Savior were stretched wide open and then nailed there, unwittingly but accurately portraying that every man, woman, and child in the entire human family is not only welcome but invited into His redeeming, exalting embrace.[13]

As the glorious Resurrection followed the agonizing Crucifixion, so blessings of every kind are poured out on those who are willing, as the Book of Mormon prophet Jacob says, to "believe in Christ, and view his death, and suffer his cross." Sometimes these blessings come soon and sometimes they come later, but the marvelous conclusion to our personal via dolorosa[14] is the promise from the Master Himself that they do and will come. To obtain such blessings, may we follow Him—unfailingly, never faltering nor fleeing, never flinching at the task, not when our crosses may be heavy and not when, for a time, the path may grow dark. For your strength, your loyalty, and your love, I give deep personal thanks. This day I bear apostolic witness of Him who was "lifted up"[15] and of the eternal blessings He bestows to those "lifted up" with Him, even the Lord Jesus Christ, amen.

Notes

1. See Jeffrey R. Holland, *Encyclopedia of Mormonism* (1992), "Atonement of Jesus Christ," 1:83.
2. Amulek speaks of the Atonement of Christ as the "great and last sacrifice," being "infinite and eternal" in its reach (Alma 34:10). For "all are fallen and are lost, and must perish except it be through the atonement" (Alma 34:9; see also verses 8–12). President John Taylor adds: "In a manner to us incomprehensible and inexplicable, [Jesus] bore the weight of the sins of the whole world; not only of Adam, but of his posterity; and in doing that, opened the kingdom of heaven, not only to all believers and all who obeyed the law of God, but to more than one-half of the human family who die before they come to years of maturity, as well as to [those] who, having died without law, will, through His mediation, be resurrected without law, and be judged without law, and thus participate . . . in the blessings of His atonement" (*An Examination into and an Elucidation of the Great Principle of the Mediation and Atonement of Our Lord and Savior Jesus Christ* [1892], 148–49; *Teachings of Presidents of the Church: John Taylor* [2001], 52–53).
3. *Teachings of Presidents of the Church: Joseph Smith* (2007), 49.
4. 1 Nephi 11:32–33.

5. 3 Nephi 27:14–15.

6. There are, of course, references to the cross in Paul's teachings (see, for example, 1 Corinthians 1:17–18; Galatians 6:14; Philippians 3:18), but these spoke to something much greater than two wooden beams nailed together or any smaller symbol of such. So when Paul speaks of the cross, he is using doctrinal shorthand to speak of the majesty of the Atonement, an arena where Latter-day Saints readily join him and quote him.

7. Early and traditional Christian figures such as Martin Luther's associate Andreas Karlstadt (1486–1541) were arguing by the late Middle Ages that "the crucifix [on its own] depicted only Christ's human suffering and neglected to display his resurrection and redemptive [powers]" (in John Hilton III, *Considering the Cross: How Calvary Connects Us with Christ* [2021], 17).

8. Harry Anderson, *The Crucifixion*; Harry Anderson, *Mary and the Resurrected Lord*.

9. See Russell M. Nelson, "Opening the Heavens for Help," *Ensign* or *Liahona*, May 2020, 72–74.

10. Gordon B. Hinckley, "The Symbol of Christ," *Ensign*, May 1975, 92.

11. Matthew 16:24.

12. 2 Samuel 24:24.

13. "His arm is extended to all people who will repent and believe on his name" (Alma 19:36; see also 2 Nephi 26:33; Alma 5:33).

14. *Via dolorosa* is a Latin phrase meaning "a painfully difficult route, passage, or series of experiences" (*Merriam-Webster.com Dictionary*, "via dolorosa"). It is most often associated with Jesus's movement from His condemnation at the hand of Pilate to His Crucifixion on Calvary.

15. See 3 Nephi 27:14–15.

HIS YOKE IS EASY
AND HIS BURDEN IS LIGHT

SISTER J. ANETTE DENNIS

First Counselor in the Relief Society General Presidency

The story is told of a man named Jack who had a beloved bird-hunting dog named Cassie. Jack was so proud of Cassie and often bragged about what a skilled dog she was. To prove this, Jack invited some friends to watch Cassie perform. After arriving at the hunting club, Jack let Cassie out to run around while he went inside to check in.

When it was time to begin, Jack was anxious to show off Cassie's amazing skills. However, Cassie was acting strangely. She wouldn't obey any of Jack's commands as she usually did so willingly. All she wanted to do was remain by his side.

Jack was frustrated and embarrassed and angry with Cassie; soon he suggested they leave. Cassie wouldn't even jump into the back of the truck, so Jack impatiently picked her up and shoved her in the kennel. He fumed as those with him made fun of his dog's behavior all the way home. Jack couldn't understand why Cassie was misbehaving. She had been trained well, and her whole desire in the past had been to please and serve him.

After arriving home, Jack began examining Cassie for injuries, burrs, or ticks, as he usually did. As he put his hand on her chest, he felt something wet and found his hand covered with blood. To his shame and horror, he found that Cassie had a long, wide gash right to her chest bone. He found another on her right front leg, also to the bone.

Jack took Cassie into his arms and began to cry. His shame at how he had misjudged and treated her was overwhelming. Cassie had been acting uncharacteristically earlier in the day because she was hurt. Her behavior had been influenced by her pain, her suffering, and her wounds. It had nothing to do with a lack of desire to obey Jack or a lack of love for him.[1]

I heard this story years ago and have never forgotten it. How many wounded individuals do we have among us? How often do we judge others based on their outward appearance and actions, or *lack* of action, when, if we fully understood, we would instead react with compassion and a desire to help instead of adding to their burdens with our judgment?

I have been guilty of this many times in my life, but the Lord has patiently taught me through personal experiences and as I have listened to the life experiences of many others. I have come to more fully appreciate the example of our dear Savior as He spent so much of *His* time ministering to others with love.

My youngest daughter's life experience has included emotional health challenges from the time she was a little girl. There have been many times throughout her life when she felt like she couldn't go on. We will be forever grateful to the earthly angels who have been there during those times: sitting with her, listening to her, crying with her, as well as sharing *together* unique gifts, spiritual understandings, and a mutual relationship of love. In such *loving* circumstances, burdens have often been lifted on *both* sides.

Elder Joseph B. Wirthlin, quoting 1 Corinthians, said, "Though I speak with the tongues of men and of angels, and have not charity, I am become as sounding brass, or a tinkling cymbal."[2]

He continued:

"Paul's message to this new body of Saints was simple and direct: Nothing you do makes much of a difference if you do not have charity. You can speak with tongues, have the gift of prophecy, understand all mysteries, and possess all knowledge; even if you have the faith to move mountains, without charity it won't profit you at all.

"'Charity is the pure love of Christ' [Moroni 7:47]. The Savior exemplified that love."[3]

In John we read, "By *this* shall all men know that ye are my disciples, *if ye have love one to another*."[4]

Many talks have been given by our Church leaders on charity, unity, love, kindness, compassion, forgiveness, and mercy. I believe the Savior is inviting us to live a higher, holier way[5]—*His* way of love where *all* can feel they truly belong and are needed.

We are commanded to *love* others,[6] not to judge them.[7] Let's lay down that heavy burden; it isn't ours to carry.[8] Instead, we can pick up the Savior's yoke of love and compassion.

"Come unto me, all ye that labour and are heavy laden, and I will give you rest.

"Take my yoke upon you, and learn of me; . . .

"For *my* yoke is easy, and *my* burden is light."[9]

The Savior does not condone sin but offers us His love and extends forgiveness when we repent. To the woman caught in adultery, He said, "Neither do *I* condemn thee: go, and sin no more."[10] Those He touched felt His *love*, and that love healed and transformed them. *His* love inspired them to *want* to change their lives. Living *His* way brings joy and peace, and He invited others to that way of living with gentleness, kindness, and love.

Elder Gary E. Stevenson said: "When we confront life's wind and rainstorms, sickness and injuries, the Lord—our Shepherd, our Caregiver—will nourish us with love and kindness. He will heal our hearts and restore our souls."[11] As followers of Jesus Christ, shouldn't we do likewise?

The Savior asks us to learn of Him[12] and do the things we have seen Him do.[13] He is the embodiment of charity, of pure love. As we incrementally learn to do what He asks of us—not out of duty or even for the blessings we might receive but purely out of love for Him and our Heavenly Father[14]—His love will flow through us and make all that He asks not only possible but eventually much easier and lighter[15] and more joyful than we could ever imagine. It will take practice; it could take years, as it has for me, but as we even desire to have love be our motivating force, He can take that desire,[16] that seed, and eventually turn it into a beautiful tree, full of the sweetest fruit.[17]

We sing in one of our beloved hymns: "Who am I to judge another when I walk imperfectly? In the quiet heart is hidden sorrow that the eye can't see."[18] Who among *us* might have hidden sorrows? The seemingly rebellious child or teenager, the children of divorce, the single mother or father, those with physical or mental health challenges, those questioning their faith, those who experience racial or cultural prejudice, those feeling alone, those longing to be married, those with unwanted addictions, and so many others dealing with a wide variety of challenging life experiences—often even those whose lives appear perfect on the surface.

None of us have perfect lives or perfect families; I certainly don't. When we seek to empathize with others who *also* experience challenges and imperfections, it can help them feel that they are not alone in *their* struggles. *Everyone* needs to feel that they really *do* belong and *are* needed in the body of Christ.[19] Satan's great desire is to divide God's children, and he has been very successful, but there is such power in unity.[20] And how we need to walk arm in arm with each other on this challenging journey of mortality!

Our prophet, President Russell M. Nelson, said: "Any *abuse* or *prejudice* toward another because of nationality, race, sexual orientation, gender, educational degrees, culture, or other significant identifiers is offensive to our Maker! Such mistreatment causes us to live beneath our stature as His covenant sons and daughters!"[21]

While President Nelson has invited all to enter and stay on the covenant path that leads back to our Father in Heaven, he also provided the following counsel: "If friends and family . . . step away from the Church, continue to love them. It is not for you to judge another's choice any more than you deserve to be criticized for staying faithful."[22]

Friends, let us remember that each person on this earth is a child of God[23] and He loves each one.[24] Are there people in *your* path who you have felt inclined to judge? If so, remember that these are valuable opportunities for us to *practice* loving as the Savior loves.[25] As we follow *His* example, we can be yoked with *Him* and help foster a feeling of love and belonging in the hearts of all our Father's children.

"We love him, because he first loved us."[26] As we are filled with the Savior's love, His yoke truly *can* be easy, and His burden *can* feel light.[27] Of this I so testify in the name of Jesus Christ, amen.

Notes

1. See Jack R. Christianson, *Healing the Wounded Soul* (2008), 27.
2. 1 Corinthians 13:1.
3. Joseph B. Wirthlin, "The Great Commandment," *Ensign* or *Liahona*, Nov. 2007, 28.
4. John 13:35, emphasis added; see also verse 34.
5. See Russell M. Nelson, "Opening Remarks," *Ensign* or *Liahona*, Nov. 2018, 6–8.
6. See Matthew 22:36–40; John 13:34–35.
7. See Dieter F. Uchtdorf, "The Merciful Obtain Mercy," *Ensign* or *Liahona*, May 2012, 70–77; see also Robert C. Gay, "Taking upon Ourselves the Name of Jesus Christ," *Ensign* or *Liahona*, Nov. 2018, 97–100.
8. An exception to this includes bishops and stake presidents. "Each bishop and stake president is 'a judge in Israel' (Doctrine and Covenants 107:72). By this authority they help members repent of sin and come unto Christ, who forgives sin (see 32.1 and 32.3)" (*General Handbook: Serving in The Church of Jesus Christ of Latter-day Saints*, 31.1.7, ChurchofJesusChrist.org).
9. Matthew 11:28–30; emphasis added.
10. John 8:11, emphasis added; see also verses 3–10.
11. Gary E. Stevenson, "Hearts Knit Together," *Liahona*, May 2021, 23.
12. See Matthew 11:29.
13. See 3 Nephi 27:21–22.
14. See Matthew 22:37–39.
15. See Mosiah 24:15.
16. See Alma 32:27.
17. See Alma 32:41.
18. "Lord, I Would Follow Thee," *Hymns*, no. 220.
19. See 1 Corinthians 12:12–27; see also Jeffrey R. Holland, "Songs Sung and Unsung," *Ensign* or *Liahona*, May 2017, 49–51.
20. See Sharon Eubank, "By Union of Feeling We Obtain Power with God," *Ensign* or *Liahona*, Nov. 2020, 55–57; see also Dale G. Renlund, "The Peace of Christ Abolishes Enmity," *Liahona*, Nov. 2021, 83–86; Sharon Eubank, "Turning Enemies into Friends" (Brigham Young University devotional, Jan. 23, 2018), speeches.byu.edu.
21. Russell M. Nelson, "Choices for Eternity" (worldwide devotional for young adults, May 15, 2022), broadcasts.ChurchofJesusChrist.org.
22. Russell M. Nelson, "Choices for Eternity," broadcasts.ChurchofJesusChrist.org.
23. See Romans 8:16.
24. See Isaiah 49:16; Romans 8:35, 38–39.
25. See Luke 6:31–38.
27. 1 John 4:19. "We are speaking here of the first great commandment given to the human family—to love God wholeheartedly, without reservation or compromise, that is, with all our heart, might, mind, and strength. This love of God is the first great *commandment* in the universe. But the first great *truth* in the universe is that *God loves us* exactly that way—wholeheartedly, without reservation or compromise, with all of *His* heart, might, mind, and strength" (Jeffrey R. Holland, "The Greatest Possession," *Liahona*, Nov. 2021, 9).
28. See Matthew 11:28–30.

HAPPY AND FOREVER

ELDER GERRIT W. GONG
Of the Quorum of the Twelve Apostles

Friends, dear brothers and sisters, do you remember believing, or wanting to believe, in happily ever after?

Then life happens. We "grow up." Relationships get complicated. This world is noisy, crowded, pushy, with pretense and posturing. Yet, in our "deep heart's core,"[1] we believe, or want to believe, somewhere, somehow, happy and forever are real and possible.

"Happy and forever" are not the imaginary stuff of fairy tales. True, enduring joy and eternity with those we love are the very essence of God's plan of happiness. His lovingly prepared way can make our eternal journey happy and forever.

We have much to celebrate and for which to be grateful. Yet, none of us is perfect, nor is any family. Our relationships include love, sociality, and personality but often also friction, hurt, sometimes profound pain.

"For as in Adam all die, even so in Christ shall all be made alive."[2] Alive in Jesus Christ includes immortality—His gift of our physical resurrection. As we live with faith and obedience, alive in Christ can also include joyfully abundant eternal life with God and those we love.

In a remarkable way, the Lord's prophet is drawing us closer to our Savior, including through sacred temple ordinances and covenants coming closer to us in more places. We have a profound opportunity and gift to discover new spiritual understanding, love, repentance, and forgiveness with each other and our families, in time and eternity.

By permission, I share two sacred, unusually spiritually direct experiences told by friends about Jesus Christ uniting families by healing even intergenerational conflict.[3] "Infinite and eternal,"[4] "stronger than the cords of death,"[5] Jesus Christ's Atonement can help us bring peace to our past and hope to our future.

When they joined The Church of Jesus Christ of Latter-day

Saints, my friend and her husband joyfully learned family relationships need not be "until death do you part." In the house of the Lord, families can be united eternally (sealed).

But my friend did not want to be sealed to her father. "He was not a nice husband to my mother. He was not a nice dad to his children," she said. "My dad will have to wait. I do not have any desire to do his temple work and be sealed with him in eternity."

For a year, she fasted, prayed, spoke a lot with the Lord about her father. Finally, she was ready. Her father's temple work was completed. Later, she said, "In my sleep my dad appeared to me in a dream, all dressed in white. He had changed. He said, 'Look at me. I am all clean. Thank you for doing the work for me in the temple.'" Her father added, "Get up and go back to the temple; your brother is waiting to be baptized."

My friend says, "My ancestors and those that have passed on are eagerly waiting for their work to be done."

"As for me," she says, "the temple is a place of healing, learning, and acknowledging the Atonement of Jesus Christ."

Second experience. Another friend researched diligently his family history. He wanted to identify his great-grandfather.

Early one morning, my friend said he felt the spiritual presence of a man in his room. The man wanted to be found and known in his family. The man felt remorse for a mistake for which he had now repented. The man helped my friend realize that my friend had no DNA connection with the person my friend thought was his great-grandfather. "In other words," my friend said, "I had discovered my great-grandfather and learned he was not the person our family records said was our great-grandfather."

His family relationships clarified, my friend said, "I feel free, at peace. It makes all the difference to know who my family are." My friend muses, "A bent branch does not mean a bad tree. How we come into this world is less important than who we are when we leave it."

The holy scriptures and sacred experiences of personal healing and peace, including with those alive in the spirit world, underscore five doctrinal principles.

First: Central in God's plan of redemption and happiness, Jesus Christ, through His Atonement, promises to unite our spirit and body, "never again to be divided, that [we] might receive a fulness of joy."[6]

Second: Atonement—at-one-ment in Christ—comes as we exercise faith and bring forth fruits unto repentance.[7] As in mortality, so in immortality. Temple ordinances do not of themselves change us or those in the spirit world. But these divine ordinances enable sanctifying covenants with the Lord, which can bring harmony with Him and each other.

Our joy becomes full as we feel Jesus Christ's grace and forgiveness for us. And as we offer the miracle of His grace and forgiveness to each other, the mercy we receive and the mercy we offer can help make life's injustices just.[8]

Third: God knows and loves us perfectly. "God is not mocked,"[9] nor can He be deceived. With perfect mercy and justice, He encircles in His arms of safety the humble and penitent.

In the Kirtland Temple, the Prophet Joseph Smith saw in vision his brother Alvin saved in the celestial kingdom. The Prophet Joseph marveled, since Alvin had died before receiving the saving ordinance of baptism.[10] Comfortingly, the Lord explained why: The Lord "will judge [us] according to [our] works, according to the desire of [our] hearts."[11] Our souls bear record of our works and desires.

Gratefully, we know the living and "the dead who repent will be redeemed, through obedience to the ordinances of the house of God"[12] and Christ's Atonement. In the spirit world, even those in sin and transgression have opportunity to repent.[13]

In contrast, those who deliberately choose wickedness, who consciously procrastinate repentance, or who in any premeditated or knowing way break the commandments, planning for easy repentance, will be judged by God and a "bright recollection of all [their] guilt."[14] We cannot knowingly sin on Saturday, then expect automatic forgiveness by partaking of the sacrament on Sunday. To missionaries or others who say following the Spirit means not having to obey mission standards or the commandments, please remember that obeying mission standards and the commandments invite the Spirit. We should none of us put off repentance. The blessings of repentance begin as we begin to repent.

Fourth: The Lord gives us divine opportunity to become more like Him as we offer proxy saving temple ordinances others need but cannot do for themselves. We become more complete and perfected[15] as we become "saviours . . . on mount Zion."[16] As we serve others, the Holy Spirit of Promise can ratify the ordinances and sanctify both giver and receiver. Both giver and receiver can make and deepen transforming covenants, over time receiving the blessings promised Abraham, Isaac, and Jacob.

Finally, fifth: As the Golden Rule[17] teaches, a sanctifying symmetry in repentance and forgiveness invites us each to offer others that which we ourselves need and desire.

Sometimes our willingness to forgive someone else enables both them and us to believe we can repent and be forgiven. Sometimes a willingness to repent and an ability to forgive come at different times. Our Savior is our Mediator with God, but He also helps bring us to ourselves and each other as we come to Him. Especially when hurt and pain are deep, repairing our relationships and healing our hearts is hard, perhaps impossible for us on our own. But heaven can give us strength and wisdom beyond our own to know when to hold on and how to let go.

We are less alone when we realize we are not alone. Our Savior always understands.[18] With our Savior's help, we can surrender our pride, our hurts, our sins to God. However we may feel as we begin, we become more whole as we trust Him to make our relationships whole.

The Lord, who sees and understands perfectly, forgives whom He will; we (being imperfect) are to forgive all. As we come to our Savior, we focus less on ourselves. We judge less and forgive more. Trusting His merits, mercy, and grace[19] can free us from contention, anger, abuse, abandonment, unfairness, and the physical and mental challenges that sometimes come with a physical body in a mortal world. Happy and forever do not mean that every relationship will be happy and forever. But a thousand millennial years when Satan is bound[20] may give us needed time and surprising ways to love, understand, and work things out as we prepare for eternity.

We find heaven's sociality in each other.[21] God's work and glory include bringing to pass happy and forever.[22] Eternal life and exaltation are to know God and Jesus Christ so, through godly power, where They are we shall be.[23]

Dear brothers and sisters, God our Heavenly Father and His Beloved Son live. They offer peace, joy, and healing to every kindred and tongue, to each of us. The Lord's prophet is leading the way. Latter-day revelation continues. May we draw closer to our Savior in the holy house of the Lord, and may He draw us closer to God and each other as we knit our hearts together in Christ-given compassion, truth, and mercy in all our generations—in time and eternity, happy and forever. In Jesus Christ, it is possible; in Jesus Christ, it is true. I so witness, in His holy name, Jesus Christ, amen.

Notes

1. William Butler Yeats, "The Lake Isle of Innisfree," in *The Norton Anthology of English Literature*, 5th ed. (1986), 1936.
2. 1 Corinthians 15:22.
3. There are many sacred experiences of hope and promises for change as we and those we love come to Jesus Christ through temple ordinances and covenants on both sides of the veil.
4. Alma 34:10.
5. Doctrine and Covenants 121:44.
6. Doctrine and Covenants 138:17.
7. See Matthew 3:8 (or Joseph Smith Translation, Matthew 3:35 [in the Bible appendix]); Luke 3:8; Alma 5:15; 12:15; 13:11–13; 34:30–33; Moroni 6:1–4; 7:25; 8:25.
8. See Alma 42:13–15; see also Robert Frost, "A Masque of Mercy," *Complete Poems of Robert Frost*, ed. by Edward Connery Lathem (1969), 521, where Frost writes, "Nothing can make injustice just but mercy."
9. Galatians 6:7.
10. See Doctrine and Covenants 137:1–6.
11. Doctrine and Covenants 137:9; see also verses 7–8, 10. Indeed, "all who have died without a knowledge of this gospel, who would have received it if they had been permitted to tarry, shall be heirs of the celestial kingdom of God." Further, the Lord continues, "All that shall die henceforth without a knowledge of it, who would have received it with all their hearts, shall be heirs of that kingdom."
12. Doctrine and Covenants 138:58.
13. See Doctrine and Covenants 138:32.
14. Alma 11:43.
15. See Doctrine and Covenants 128:15 and footnote *b* in Matthew 5:48, which shows the Greek translation for *perfect* as "complete, finished, fully developed."

16. Obadiah 1:21.
17. See Matthew 7:12.
18. "He [was] despised and rejected of men; a man of sorrows, and acquainted with grief" (Isaiah 53:3), but also a Man who gathered the little children and wept with a joy that was full (see 3 Nephi 17:20–24).
19. See 2 Nephi 2:8.
20. See Doctrine and Covenants 43:30–31. 1 Nephi 22:26 reminds us that Satan's power will be limited in the Millennium "because of the righteousness of [the Lord's] people."
21. See Doctrine and Covenants 130:2.
22. See Moses 1:39.
23. See Doctrine and Covenants 132:23–24; see also Doctrine and Covenants 29:29, which says, "For where I am they cannot come, for they have no power."

PATTERNS OF DISCIPLESHIP

ELDER JOSEPH W. SITATI
Emeritus Member of the Seventy

Pattern of Faith

This morning our two children and three grandchildren in North America, and about half of the world, saw the brightness of the sun rising majestically in the east. The other three children and seven grandchildren in Africa, and the other half of the world, saw darkness gradually creep upon them as the sun sank over the horizon in the west.

This timeless constancy of the onset of day and night is one daily reminder of realities that govern our lives that we cannot change. When we respect and align what we do with these eternal realities, we experience internal peace and harmony. When we don't, we are unsettled, and things do not work as we expect.

Day and night is one example of patterns that God has given to everyone who has ever lived on the earth, of things as they really are. It is an absolute truth of our human existence that we cannot negotiate around according to our own desires and get away with it. I am reminded of this every time I take a flight from Africa to come to general conference, resetting the body clock backward by 10 hours in one day.

Whenever we care to notice, we see that Heavenly Father has given us sufficient witnesses of truth to govern our lives so we will know Him and have the blessings of peace and joy.

Through the Prophet Joseph Smith, the Spirit of the Lord affirms, "And again, I will give unto you a pattern in all things, that ye may not be deceived; for Satan is abroad in the land, and he goeth forth deceiving the nations."[1]

Korihor the anti-Christ fell for such deception, disbelieving the existence of God and the coming of Christ. To him the prophet Alma testified, "All things denote there is a God; yea, even the earth, and all things that are upon the face of it, yea, and its motion, yea, and also all the planets which move in their regular form do witness that there is a Supreme Creator."[2]

When Korihor insisted to be given a sign before he could believe, Alma caused him to be struck dumb. Humbled by his affliction, Korihor freely confessed to having been deceived by the devil.

We do not need to be deceived. The miracle of intelligent life constantly plays before us. And a brief gaze and reflection upon the wonders of the heavens arrayed with numberless stars and galaxies prompt the soul of the believing heart to proclaim, "My God, how great thou art!"[3]

Yes, God our Heavenly Father lives, and He manifests Himself to us all the time in multiple ways.

Pattern of Humility

But to acknowledge, believe, and continue in God, our hearts need to be receptive to the Spirit of truth. Alma taught that faith is preceded by humility.[4] Mormon added that it is impossible for anyone who is not "meek and lowly in heart" to have faith and hope and to receive the Spirit of God.[5] King Benjamin declared that anyone who prioritizes the glory of the world is "an enemy to God."[6]

By submitting to baptism to fulfill all righteousness, even though He was righteous and holy, Jesus Christ demonstrated that humility before God is a foundational attribute of His disciples.[7]

All new disciples are required to demonstrate humility before God through the ordinance of baptism. Thus, "all those who humble themselves before God, and desire to be baptized, and come forth with broken hearts and contrite spirits . . . shall be received by baptism into his church."[8]

Humility inclines the heart of the disciple toward repentance and obedience. The Spirit of God is then able to bring truth to that heart, and it will find entry.[9]

It is a lack of humility that contributes most to the fulfillment of the Apostle Paul's prophecy in these last days:

"For men shall be lovers of their own selves, covetous, boasters, proud, blasphemers, disobedient to parents, unthankful, unholy,

"Without natural affection, trucebreakers, false accusers, incontinent, fierce, despisers of those that are good."[10]

The invitation of the Savior to learn of Him is an invitation to turn away from the enticings of worldliness and to become as He is—meek and lowly of heart, humble. We are then able to take up His yoke and discover that it is easy—that discipleship is not a burden but a joy, as President Russell M. Nelson has so eloquently and repeatedly taught us.

Pattern of Love

Learning about Christ and His ways leads us to know and to love Him.

He showed by example that with an attitude of humility it is indeed possible to know and to love God the Father with all our being and to love others as we love ourselves, holding back nothing. His ministry on earth, during which He put both His will and His body on the altar, was a pattern for the application of these principles on which His gospel is founded. Both principles are outward looking and are about how we relate to others, not about seeking personal gratification or glory.

The miraculous irony of it is that when we focus our best efforts on loving God and others, we are enabled to discover our own true divine worth as sons and daughters of God, with the complete peace and joy that this experience brings.

We become one with God and with one another through love and service. Then we can receive the witness of the Holy Ghost of that pure love, the fruit which Lehi speaks about as "most sweet, above all that [he] ever before tasted."[11]

The crown that Christ received by giving and doing all in His ability to set the pattern of loving the Father and loving us was to receive all power, even all that the Father has, which is exaltation.[12]

Our opportunity to nurture in our souls a lasting love of God and of our neighbor starts at home with the holy habits of connecting with the Father daily in personal and family prayer in the name of His Only Begotten Son, learning together of Them through individual and family scripture study, observing the Sabbath day together, and individually holding a current temple recommend, using it together as often as we are able.

As we each individually grow in our knowledge and love of the Father and the Son, we grow in appreciation and love for one another. Our ability to love and serve others outside the home is greatly enhanced.

What we do at home is the true crucible of enduring and joyful discipleship. The sweetest blessings of the restored gospel that my wife, Gladys, and I have enjoyed in our household have come from learning to know and to honor God at home and to share His love with our posterity.

Pattern of Service

Love for God and service to one another nurtured at home and service to others outside the home in time grow into the attribute of charity.

This resonates with the pattern of consecrated service in the kingdom of God that is set before us by the Lord's living prophets and apostles. We become one with them.

We are then enabled to look, through them, unto the Lord "in every thought," so that we shall "doubt not" and "fear not."[13]

Like the Lord's living prophets and apostles, we can go forth with "bowels . . . full of charity towards all men, and to the household of faith, [with] virtue [garnishing our] thoughts unceasingly; . . . [and our] confidence [waxing] strong in the presence of God; and the doctrine of the priesthood . . . [distilling] upon [our souls] as the dews from heaven."

With the Lord's living prophets and apostles, we too can join a virtuous circle of faith strengthened by consecrated service in which "the Holy Ghost [is our] constant companion, [our] scepter [is] an unchanging scepter of righteousness and truth; and [our] dominion [is] an everlasting dominion, and without compulsory means it [flows] unto [us] forever and ever."[14] For this is the promise of the Father's plan. In the name of Jesus Christ, amen.

Notes

1. Doctrine and Covenants 52:14.
2. Alma 30:44.
3. "How Great Thou Art," *Hymns,* no 86.
4. See Alma 32:14–21.
5. See Moroni 7:42–44.
6. Mosiah 3:19.
7. See 2 Nephi 31:6–7.
8. Doctrine and Covenants 20:37.
9. See 2 Nephi 33:1.
10. 2 Timothy 3:2–3.
11. 1 Nephi 8:11.
12. See Matthew 28:18; Doctrine and Covenants 84:38.
13. Doctrine and Covenants 6:36.
14. Doctrine and Covenants 121:45–46.

LASTING DISCIPLESHIP

PRESIDENT STEVEN J. LUND

Young Men General President

During this past summer, over 200,000 of our young people all over the world grew in faith at one of the hundreds of weeklong sessions of For the Strength of Youth, or FSY, conferences. Coming out of pandemic isolation, for many it was an act of faith in the Lord to even attend. Many of the young participants seem to follow a similar upward arc toward deeper conversion. At the end of their week, I liked to ask them, "So, how's it been?"

They sometimes said something like this: "Well, on Monday I was so annoyed with my mother because she made me come and do this. And I didn't know anybody. And I didn't think it was for me. And I wouldn't have any friends. . . . But now it's Friday, and I just want to stay here. I just want to feel the Spirit in my life. I want to live like this."

They each have their own stories to tell of moments of clarity and of spiritual gifts washing through them and carrying them along that arc of growth. I too was changed by this summer of FSY as I have seen the Spirit of God relentlessly responding to the righteous desires of the individual hearts of these young multitudes who individually found the courage to trust Him with a week in His keeping.

Like brightly hulled steel ships at sea, we live in a spiritually corrosive environment where the most gleaming convictions must be mindfully maintained or they can become etched, then corrode, and then crumble away.

What Kinds of Things Can We Do to Maintain the Fire of Our Convictions?

Experiences like FSY conferences, camps, sacrament meetings, and missions can help to burnish our testimonies, taking us through arcs of growth and spiritual discovery to places of relative peace. But what must we do to stay there and continue to "press forward with a steadfastness in Christ" (2 Nephi 31:20) rather than slipping backward? We must continue to do those things that brought us there in the first place, like praying often, drenching ourselves in scripture, and serving sincerely.

For some of us, it may require an exercise of trusting in the Lord even to attend sacrament meeting. But once we are there, the healing influence of the Lord's sacrament, infusions of gospel principles, and the nurture of the Church community can send us home on higher ground.

Where Does the Power in Gathering Together in Person Come From?

At FSY, a couple of hundred thousand and more of our youth came to better know the Savior by using a simple formula of coming together where two or more of them were gathered in His name (see Matthew 18:20), engaging the gospel and the scriptures, singing together, praying together, and finding peace in Christ. This is a powerful prescription for spiritual awakening.

This far-flung band of brothers and sisters has now gone home to determine what it means to still "trust in the Lord" (Proverbs 3:5; 2022 youth theme) when swept up in the cacophony of a rambunctious world. It is one thing to "hear Him" (Joseph Smith—History 1:17) in a quiet place of contemplation with scriptures wide open. But it is quite another thing to carry our discipleship into this mortal flurry of distractions, where we must strive to "hear Him" even through the blur of self-concern and faltering confidence. Let there be no doubt: it is the very stuff of heroes displayed by our youth when they set their hearts and minds to standing upright against the shifting moral tectonics of our time.

What Can Families Do at Home to Build on the Momentum Created at Church Activities?

I once served as husband to the stake Young Women president. One night I was tasked with arranging cookies in the foyer while my wife was conducting a fireside in the chapel for parents and their daughters preparing to attend Young Women camp the next week. After explaining where to be and what to bring, she said, "Now,

Tuesday morning when you drop your sweet girls off at the bus, you hug them tight. And you kiss them goodbye—because they are not coming back."

I heard someone gasp, then realized it was me. "Not coming back?"

But then she continued: "When you drop off those Tuesday-morning girls, they will leave behind the distractions of lesser things and spend a week together learning and growing and trusting in the Lord. We will pray together and sing and cook and serve together and share testimonies together and do the things that allow us to feel Heavenly Father's Spirit, all week long, until it soaks all the way into our bones. And on Saturday, those girls that you see getting off that bus will not be the ones you dropped off on Tuesday. They will be new creatures. And if you help them continue from that higher plane, they will astonish you. They will continue to change and to grow. And so will your family."

On that Saturday, it was just as she predicted. As I was loading tents, I heard my wife's voice in the little woodsy amphitheater where the girls had gathered before heading for home. I heard her say, "Oh, there you are. We've been watching for you all week. Our Saturday girls."

The stalwart youth of Zion are voyaging through stunning times. Finding joy *in* this world of prophesied disruption without becoming part *of* that world, with its blind spot toward holiness, is their particular charge. About a hundred years ago, G. K. Chesterton spoke almost as though he saw this quest as being home centered and Church supported when he said, "We have to feel the universe at once as an ogre's castle, to be stormed, and yet as our own cottage, to which we can return at evening" (*Orthodoxy* [1909], 130).

Thankfully, they do not have to go out into battle alone. They have each other. And they have you. And they follow a living prophet, President Russell M. Nelson, who leads with the knowing optimism of a seer in proclaiming that the great endeavor of these times—the gathering of Israel—will be both grand and majestic (see "Hope of Israel" [worldwide youth devotional, June 3, 2018], HopeofIsrael.ChurchofJesusChrist.org).

This summer, my wife, Kalleen, and I were changing planes in Amsterdam where, many years earlier, I was a new missionary. After I had spent months struggling to learn Dutch, our KLM flight was landing, and the captain made an incoherent announcement over the PA system. After a moment of silence, my companion mumbled, "I think that was Dutch." We glanced up, reading each other's thoughts: All was lost.

But all was not lost. As I marveled over the leaps of faith we had then taken as we walked through this airport on our way to the miracles that would rain down upon us as missionaries, I was abruptly brought back to the present by a living, breathing missionary who was boarding a plane home. He introduced himself and asked, "President Lund, what do I do now? What do I do to remain strong?"

Well, this is the same question that is on the minds of our youth when they leave FSY conferences, youth camps, and temple trips and anytime they feel the powers of heaven: "How can loving God turn into lasting discipleship?"

I felt an upwelling of love for this clear-eyed missionary serving the last hours of his mission, and in that momentary stillness of the Spirit, I heard my voice crack as I said simply, "You don't have to wear the badge to bear His name."

I wanted to put my hands on his shoulders and say, "Here's what you do. You go home, and you just be *this*. You are so good you almost glow in the dark. Your mission discipline and sacrifices have made you a magnificent son of God. Keep doing at home what has worked so powerfully for you here. You have learned to pray and to whom you pray and the language of prayer. You have studied His words and come to love the Savior by trying to be like Him. You have loved Heavenly Father like He loved His Father, served others like He served others, and lived the commandments like He lived them—and when you didn't, you have repented. Your discipleship isn't just a slogan on a T-shirt—it has become a part of your life purposefully lived for others. So you go home, and you do that. Be that. Carry this spiritual momentum into the rest of your life."

I know that through trusting in the Lord Jesus Christ and His covenant path, we can find spiritual confidence and peace as we nurture holy habits and righteous routines that can sustain and fuel the fires of our faith. May we each move ever closer to those warming fires and, come what may, remain. In the name of Jesus Christ, amen.

PUT ON THY STRENGTH, O ZION

ELDER DAVID A. BEDNAR
Of the Quorum of the Twelve Apostles

Parables are a defining feature of the Lord Jesus Christ's masterful approach to teaching. Simply defined, the Savior's parables are stories used to compare spiritual truths with material things and mortal experiences. For example, the New Testament Gospels are replete with teachings likening the kingdom of heaven to a grain of mustard seed,[1] to a pearl of great price,[2] to a householder and laborers in his vineyard,[3] to ten virgins,[4] and to many other things. During part of the Lord's Galilean ministry, the scriptures indicate that "without a parable spake he not unto them."[5]

The intended meaning or message of a parable typically is not expressed explicitly. Rather, the story only conveys divine truth to a receiver in proportion to his or her faith in God, personal spiritual preparation, and willingness to learn. Thus, an individual must exercise moral agency and actively "ask, seek, and knock"[6] to discover the truths embedded in a parable.

I earnestly pray that the Holy Ghost will enlighten each of us as we now consider the importance of the parable of the royal marriage feast.

The Royal Marriage Feast

"And Jesus . . . spake unto them again by parables, and said,

"The kingdom of heaven is like unto a certain king, which made a marriage for his son,

"And sent forth his servants to call them that were bidden to the wedding: and they would not come.

"Again, he sent forth other servants, saying, Tell them which are bidden, Behold, I have prepared my dinner: my oxen and my fatlings are killed, and all things are ready: come unto the marriage.

"But they made light of it, and went their ways, one to his farm, another to his merchandise."[7]

In ancient times, one of the most joyous occasions in Jewish life was a wedding celebration—an event that would span a week or even two. Such an event required extensive planning, and guests were informed far in advance, with a reminder sent on the opening day of the festivities. An invitation from a king to his subjects to a wedding such as this was essentially considered a command. Yet, many of the bidden guests in this parable did not come.[8]

"The refusal to attend the king's feast was a deliberate [act of] rebellion against . . . royal authority and a personal indignity against both the reigning sovereign and his son. . . . The turning away by one man to his farm and by another to his [business interests]"[9] reflects their misguided priorities and total disregard of the king's will.[10]

The parable continues:

"Then saith he to his servants, The wedding is ready, but they which were bidden were not worthy.

"Go ye therefore into the highways, and as many as ye shall find, bid to the marriage.

"So those servants went out into the highways, and gathered together all as many as they found, both bad and good: and the wedding was furnished with guests."[11]

The custom in those days was for the host of a wedding feast—in this parable, the king—to provide garments for the wedding guests. Such wedding garments were simple, nondescript robes that all attendees wore. In this way, rank and station were eliminated, and everyone at the feast could mingle as equals.[12]

People invited from the highways to attend the wedding would not have had the time or means to procure appropriate attire in preparation for the event. Consequently, the king likely gave guests the garments from his own wardrobe. Everyone was given the opportunity to clothe themselves in garments of royalty.[13]

As the king entered the wedding hall, he surveyed the audience and immediately noticed that one conspicuous guest was not wearing a wedding garment. The man was brought forward, and the king asked, "Friend, how camest thou in hither not having a wedding garment? And he was speechless."[14] In essence, the king asked, "Why are you not wearing a wedding garment, even though one was provided for you?"[15]

The man obviously was not dressed properly for this special occasion, and the phrase "And he was speechless" indicates that the man was without excuse.[16]

Elder James E. Talmage provides this instructive commentary about the significance of the man's actions: "That the unrobed guest was guilty of neglect, intentional disrespect, or some more grievous offense, is plain from the context. The king at first was graciously considerate, inquiring only as to how the man had entered without a wedding garment. Had the guest been able to explain his exceptional appearance, or had he any reasonable excuse to offer, he surely would have spoken; but we are told that he remained speechless. The king's summons had been freely extended to all whom his servants had found; but each of them had to enter the royal palace by the door; and before reaching the banquet room, in which the king would appear in person, each would be properly attired; but the deficient one, by some means had entered by another way; and not having passed the attendant sentinels at the portal, he was an intruder."[17]

A Christian author, John O. Reid, noted that the man's refusal to wear the wedding garment exemplified blatant "disrespect for both the king and his son." He did not simply lack a wedding garment; rather, he chose not to wear one. He rebelliously refused to dress appropriately for the occasion. The king's reaction was swift and decisive: "Bind him hand and foot, and take him away, and cast him into outer darkness; there shall be weeping and gnashing of teeth."[18]

The king's judgment of the man is not based primarily upon the lack of a wedding garment—but that "he was, in fact, determined not to wear one. The man . . . desired the honor of attending the wedding feast, but . . . did not want to follow the custom of the king. He wanted to do things his own way. His lack of proper dress revealed his inner rebellion against the king and his instructions."[19]

Many Are Called, but Few Are Chosen

The parable then concludes with this penetrating scripture: "For many are called, but few are chosen."[20]

Interestingly, Joseph Smith made the following adjustment to this verse from Matthew in his inspired translation of the Bible: "For many are called, but few are chosen; *wherefore all do not have on the wedding garment.*"[21]

The *invitation to* the wedding feast and the *choice to partake in* the feast are related but different. The invitation is to all men and women. An individual may even accept the invitation and sit down at the feast—yet not be chosen to partake because he or she does not have the appropriate wedding garment of converting faith in the Lord Jesus and His divine grace. Thus, we have both God's call and our individual response to that call, and many may be called but few chosen.[22]

To be or to become chosen is not an exclusive status conferred upon us. Rather, you and I ultimately can choose to be chosen through the righteous exercise of our moral agency.

Please note the use of the word *chosen* in the following familiar verses from the Doctrine and Covenants:

"Behold, there are many called, but few are *chosen*. And why are they not *chosen*?

"Because their hearts are set so much upon the things of this world, and aspire to the honors of men."[23]

I believe the implication of these verses is quite straightforward. God does not have a list of favorites to which we must hope our names will someday be added. He does not limit "the chosen" to a restricted few. Instead, *our* hearts, *our* desires, *our* honoring of sacred gospel covenants and ordinances, *our* obedience to the commandments, and, most importantly, the Savior's redeeming grace and mercy determine whether we are counted as one of God's chosen.[24]

"For we labor diligently to write, to persuade our children, and also our brethren, to believe in Christ, and to be reconciled to God; for we know that it is by grace that we are saved, after all we can do."[25]

In the busyness of our daily lives and in the commotion of the contemporary world in which we live, we may be distracted from the eternal things that matter the most by making pleasure, prosperity, popularity, and prominence our primary priorities. Our short-term preoccupation with "the things of this world" and "the honors of men" may lead us to forfeit our spiritual birthright for far less than a mess of pottage.[26]

Promise and Testimony

I repeat the admonition of the Lord to His people delivered through the Old Testament prophet Haggai: "Now therefore thus saith the Lord of hosts; Consider your ways."[27]

Each of us should evaluate our temporal and spiritual priorities sincerely and prayerfully to identify the things in our lives that may impede the bounteous blessings that Heavenly Father and the Savior are willing to bestow upon us. And surely the Holy Ghost will help us to see ourselves as we really are.[28]

As we appropriately seek for the spiritual gift of eyes to see and ears to hear,[29] I promise that we will be blessed with the capacity and judgment to strengthen our covenant connection with the living Lord. We also will receive the power of godliness in our lives[30]—and ultimately be both called to and chosen for the Lord's feast.

"Awake, awake; put on thy strength, O Zion."[31]

"For Zion must increase in beauty, and in holiness; her borders must be enlarged; her stakes must be strengthened; yea, verily I say unto you, Zion must arise and put on her beautiful garments."[32]

I joyfully declare my witness of the divinity and living reality of God, our Eternal Father, and of His Beloved Son, Jesus Christ. I testify that Jesus Christ is our Savior and Redeemer and that He lives. And I also witness that the Father and the Son appeared to the boy Joseph Smith, thus initiating the Restoration of the Savior's gospel in the latter days. May each of us seek for and be blessed with eyes to see and ears to hear, I pray in the sacred name of the Lord Jesus Christ, amen.

Notes

1. See Matthew 13:31–32.
2. See Matthew 13:45–46.
3. See Matthew 20:1–16.

4. See Matthew 25:1–13.
5. Mark 4:34.
6. See Matthew 7:7–8; Luke 11:9–10.
7. Matthew 22:1–5.
8. See James E. Talmage, *Jesus the Christ* (1916), 536–40.
9. James E. Talmage, *Jesus the Christ*, 537.
10. See James E. Talmage, *Jesus the Christ*, 537.
11. Matthew 22:8–10.
12. See John O. Reid, "Many Are Called, Few Are Chosen," *Forerunner*, Mar.–Apr. 2016, 8, cgg.org.
13. See Joseph Fielding McConkie, *Gospel Symbolism* (1985), 132.
14. Matthew 22:12.
15. See Reid, "Many Are Called, Few Are Chosen," 8.
16. See Reid, "Many Are Called, Few Are Chosen," 8.
17. James E. Talmage, *Jesus the Christ*, 539–40.
18. Matthew 22:13; see Reid, "Many Are Called, Few Are Chosen," 8.
19. Reid, "Many Are Called, Few Are Chosen," 8.
20. Matthew 22:14.
21. Joseph Smith Translation, Matthew 22:14 (in Matthew 22:14, footnote *b*); emphasis added.
22. See Alfred Edersheim, *The Life and Times of Jesus the Messiah* (1993), 769–71.
23. Doctrine and Covenants 121:34–35; emphasis added.
24. See David A. Bednar, "The Tender Mercies of the Lord," *Ensign* or *Liahona*, May 2005, 99–102.
25. 2 Nephi 25:23.
26. See Genesis 25:29–34.
27. Haggai 1:5.
28. See Jacob 4:13; Doctrine and Covenants 93:24.
29. See Matthew 13:16.
30. See Doctrine and Covenants 84:19–21.
31. Isaiah 52:1.
32. Doctrine and Covenants 82:14.

OVERCOME THE WORLD AND FIND REST

PRESIDENT RUSSELL M. NELSON

President of The Church of Jesus Christ of Latter-day Saints

My dear brothers and sisters, I am grateful to greet you on this glorious Sabbath morning. You are constantly on my mind. I marvel at the way you spring into action whenever you see others in need. I stand amazed at the faith and testimony you demonstrate again and again. I weep over your heartaches, disappointments, and worries. I love you. I assure you that our Heavenly Father and His Beloved Son, Jesus Christ, love you. They are intimately aware of your circumstances, your goodness, your needs, and your prayers for help. Again and again, I pray for you to feel Their love for you.

Experiencing Their love is vital, as it seems that we are accosted daily by an onslaught of sobering news. You may have had days when you wished you could don your pajamas, curl up in a ball, and ask someone to awaken you when the turmoil is over.

But, my dear brothers and sisters, so many wonderful things are ahead. In coming days, we will see the *greatest* manifestations of the Savior's power that the world has *ever* seen. Between now and the time He returns "with power and great glory,"[1] He will bestow countless privileges, blessings, and miracles upon the faithful.

Nonetheless, we are presently living in what surely is a most complicated time in the history of the world. The complexities and challenges leave many people feeling overwhelmed and exhausted. However, consider a recent experience that might shed light on how you and I can find rest.

During the recent open house of the Washington D.C. Temple, a member of the open house committee witnessed an insightful interchange as he escorted several prominent journalists through the temple. Somehow a young family became attached to this media tour. One reporter kept asking about the "journey" of a temple patron as he or she moves through the temple. He wanted to know if the temple journey is symbolic of the challenges in a person's journey through life.

A young boy in the family picked up on the conversation. When the tour group entered an endowment room, the boy pointed to the altar, where people kneel to make covenants with God, and said, "Oh, that's nice. Here is a place for people to *rest* on their temple journey."

I doubt that the boy knew just how profound his observation was. He likely had no idea about the direct connection between making a covenant with God in the temple and the Savior's stunning promise:

"Come unto me, all ye that labour and are heavy laden, and I will give you *rest*.

"Take my yoke upon you, and learn of me; . . . and ye shall find *rest* unto your souls.

"For my yoke is easy, and my burden is light."[2]

Dear brothers and sisters, I grieve for those who leave the Church because they feel membership requires too much of them. They have not yet discovered that making and keeping covenants actually makes life easier! Each person who makes covenants in baptismal fonts and in temples—and keeps them—has increased access to the power of Jesus Christ. Please ponder that stunning truth!

The reward for keeping covenants with God is heavenly power—power that strengthens us to withstand our trials, temptations, and heartaches better. This power eases our way. Those who live the higher laws of Jesus Christ have access to His higher power. Thus, covenant keepers are entitled to a special kind of *rest* that comes to them through their covenantal relationship with God.

Before the Savior submitted Himself to the agony of Gethsemane and Calvary, He declared to His Apostles, "In the world ye shall have tribulation: but be of good cheer; I have *overcome the world*."[3] Subsequently, Jesus entreated each of us to do the same when He said, "I *will* that *ye* should *overcome* the world."[4]

Dear brothers and sisters, my message to you today is that because Jesus Christ overcame this fallen world, and because He atoned for each of us, you too can overcome this sin-saturated, self-centered, and often exhausting world.

Because the Savior, through His infinite Atonement, redeemed each of us from weakness, mistakes, and sin, and because He experienced every pain, worry, and burden you have ever had,[5] then as you truly repent and seek His help, you can rise above this present precarious world.

You can overcome the spiritually and emotionally exhausting plagues of the world, including arrogance, pride, anger, immorality, hatred, greed, jealousy, and fear. Despite the distractions and distortions that swirl around us, you can find true *rest*—meaning relief and peace—even amid your most vexing problems.

This important truth prompts three fundamental questions:

First, what does it mean to overcome the world?

Second, how do we do it?

And third, how does overcoming the world bless our lives?

What does it mean to overcome the world? It means overcoming the temptation to care more about the things of this world than the things of God. It means trusting the doctrine of Christ more than the philosophies of men. It means delighting in truth, denouncing deception, and becoming "humble followers of Christ."[6] It means choosing to refrain from anything that drives the Spirit away. It means being willing to "give away" even our favorite sins.[7]

Now, overcoming the world certainly does not mean becoming perfect in this life, nor does it mean that your problems will magically evaporate—because they won't. And it does *not* mean that you won't still make mistakes. But overcoming the world does mean that your resistance to sin will increase. Your heart will soften as your faith in Jesus Christ increases.[8] Overcoming the world means growing to love God and His Beloved Son more than you love anyone or anything else.

How, then, do we overcome the world? King Benjamin taught us how. He said that "the natural man is an enemy to God" and remains so forever "*unless* he yields to the enticings of the Holy Spirit, and putteth off the natural man and becometh a saint through the atonement of Christ the Lord."[9] Each time you seek for and follow the promptings of the Spirit, each time you do anything good—things that "the natural man" would not do—you are overcoming the world.

Overcoming the world is not an event that happens in a day or two. It happens over a lifetime as we repeatedly embrace the doctrine of Christ. We cultivate faith in Jesus Christ by repenting daily and keeping covenants that endow us with power. We stay on the covenant path and are blessed with spiritual strength, personal revelation, increasing faith, and the ministering of angels. Living the doctrine of Christ can produce the most powerful virtuous cycle, creating spiritual momentum in our lives.[10]

As we strive to live the higher laws of Jesus Christ, our hearts and our very natures begin to change. The Savior *lifts* us above the pull of this fallen world by blessing us with greater charity, humility, generosity, kindness, self-discipline, peace, and *rest*.

Now, you may be thinking this sounds more like hard spiritual work than *rest*. But here is the grand truth: while the world insists that power, possessions, popularity, and pleasures of the flesh bring happiness, they do not! They cannot! What they do produce is nothing but a hollow substitute for "the blessed and happy state of those [who] keep the commandments of God."[11]

The truth is that it is much *more exhausting* to seek happiness where you can *never* find it! However, when you yoke yourself to Jesus Christ and do the spiritual work required to overcome the world, He, and He alone, does have the power to lift you above the pull of this world.

Now, how does overcoming the world bless our lives? The answer is clear: entering into a covenant relationship with God binds us to Him in a way that makes *everything* about life easier. Please do not misunderstand me: I did *not* say that making covenants makes life *easy*. In fact, expect opposition, because the adversary does not want you to discover the power of Jesus Christ. But yoking yourself with the Savior means you have access to *His* strength and redeeming power.

I reaffirm a profound teaching of President Ezra Taft Benson: "Men and women who turn their lives over to God will discover that He can make a lot more out of their lives than they can. He will deepen their joys, expand their vision, quicken their minds, . . . lift their spirits, multiply their blessings, increase their opportunities, comfort their souls, raise up friends, and pour out peace."[12]

These incomparable privileges follow those who seek the support of heaven to help them overcome this world. To this end, I extend to members of the entire Church the same charge I gave to our young adults last May. I urged them then—and I *plead* with you now—to take charge of your own testimony of Jesus Christ and His gospel. Work for it. Nurture it so that it will grow. Feed it truth. Don't pollute it with false philosophies of unbelieving men and women. As you make the continual strengthening of your testimony of Jesus Christ your highest priority, watch for miracles to happen in your life.[13]

My plea to you this morning is to find *rest* from the intensity, uncertainty, and anguish of this world by *overcoming* the world through your covenants with God. Let Him know through your prayers and your actions that you are serious about overcoming the world. Ask Him to enlighten your mind and send the help you need. Each day, record the thoughts that come to you as you pray; then follow through diligently. Spend more time in the temple, and seek to understand how the temple teaches you to rise above this fallen world.[14]

As I have stated before, the gathering of Israel is the *most* important work taking place on earth today. One crucial element of this gathering is preparing a people who are able, ready, and worthy to receive the Lord when He comes again, a people who have already chosen Jesus Christ over this fallen world, a people who rejoice in their agency to live the higher, holier laws of Jesus Christ.

I call upon you, my dear brothers and sisters, to become this righteous people. Cherish and honor your covenants above all other commitments. As you let God prevail in your life, I promise you greater peace, confidence, joy, and yes, *rest*.

With the power of the holy apostleship vested in me, I bless you in your quest to overcome this world. I bless you to increase your faith in Jesus Christ and learn better how to draw upon His power. I bless you to be able to discern truth from error. I bless you to care more about the things of God than the things of this world. I bless you to see the needs of those around you and strengthen those you love. Because Jesus Christ overcame this world, you can too. I so testify in the sacred name of Jesus Christ, amen.

Notes

1. Joseph Smith—Matthew 1:36: "Then shall appear the sign of the Son of Man in heaven, and then shall all the tribes of the earth mourn; and they shall see the Son of Man coming in the clouds of heaven, with power and great glory."
2. Matthew 11:28–30; emphasis added.
3. John 16:33; emphasis added.
4. Doctrine and Covenants 64:2; emphasis added.
5. See Alma 7:11–13.
6. 2 Nephi 28:14.
7. See the account of King Lamoni's father in Alma 22, especially Alma 22:18.
8. See Mosiah 5:7.
9. Mosiah 3:19; emphasis added.
10. See 2 Nephi 31; 3 Nephi 27:16–20.
11. Mosiah 2:41.
12. *Teachings of Presidents of the Church: Ezra Taft Benson* (2014), 42–43.
13. See Russell M. Nelson, "Choices for Eternity" (worldwide devotional for young adults, May 15, 2022), broadcasts.ChurchofJesusChrist.org.
14. President David O. McKay said that in the temple we take a "step-by-step ascent into the Eternal Presence" (in Truman G. Madsen, *The Temple: Where Heaven Meets Earth* [2008], 11).

SUNDAY AFTERNOON SESSION

OCTOBER 2, 2022

LEGACY OF ENCOURAGEMENT

PRESIDENT HENRY B. EYRING

Second Counselor in the First Presidency

My dear brothers and sisters, I am grateful to be gathered with you in this general conference of The Church of Jesus Christ of Latter-day Saints. We have felt your faith and your love wherever you are. We have been edified by the inspired teaching, the powerful testimonies, and the magnificent music.

I encourage you to continue striving to qualify to return to Heavenly Father and Jesus Christ. Wherever you are on the covenant path, you will find a struggle against the physical trials of mortality and the opposition of Satan.

As my mother told me when I complained of how hard something was, "Oh, Hal, of course it's hard. It's supposed to be. Life is a test."

She could say that calmly, even with a smile, because she knew two things. Regardless of the struggle, what would matter most would be to arrive at home to be with her Heavenly Father. And she knew she could do it through faith in her Savior.

She felt that He was close to her. In the days she knew she was about to die, she talked with me about the Savior as she lay in her bedroom. There was a door to another room near her bed. She smiled and looked at the door when she spoke calmly of seeing Him soon. I still remember looking at the door and imagining the room behind it.

She is now in the spirit world. She was able to keep her eyes on the prize she wanted despite years of physical and personal trial.

The legacy of encouragement she left for us is best described in Moroni 7, where Mormon encourages his son Moroni and his people. It is a legacy of encouragement to a posterity as was my mother's to her family. Mormon passed that legacy of encouragement to all who have a determination to qualify, through all their mortal tests, for eternal life.

Mormon begins in the first verses of Moroni 7 with a testimony of Jesus Christ, of angels, and of the Spirit of Christ, which allows us to know good from evil and so be able to choose the right.

He puts Jesus Christ first, as do all who succeed in giving encouragement to those struggling upward on the path to their heavenly home:

"For no man can be saved, according to the words of Christ, save they shall have faith in his name; wherefore, if these things have ceased, then has faith ceased also; and awful is the state of man, for they are as though there had been no redemption made.

"But behold, my beloved brethren, I judge better things of you, for I judge that ye have faith in Christ because of your meekness; for if ye have not faith in him then ye are not fit to be numbered among the people of his church."[1]

Mormon saw meekness as evidence of the strength of their faith. He saw that they felt dependent on the Savior. He encouraged them by noting *that* faith. Mormon continued giving them encouragement by helping them see that their faith and meekness would build their assurance and their confidence of success in their struggle:

"And again, my beloved brethren, I would speak unto you concerning hope. How is it that ye can attain unto faith, save ye shall have hope?

"And what is it that ye shall hope for? Behold I say unto you that ye shall have hope through the atonement of Christ and the power of his resurrection, to be raised unto life eternal, and this because of your faith in him according to the promise.

"Wherefore, if a man have faith he must needs have hope; for without faith there cannot be any hope.

"And again, behold I say unto you that he cannot have faith and hope, save he shall be meek, and lowly of heart."[2]

Mormon then encourages them by testifying that they are on the way to receiving the gift of their hearts being filled with the pure love of Christ. He weaves together for them the interactions of faith in Jesus Christ, meekness, humility, the Holy Ghost, and the firm hope of receiving eternal life. He encourages them this way:

"For none is acceptable before God, save the meek and lowly

in heart; and if a man be meek and lowly in heart, and confesses by the power of the Holy Ghost that Jesus is the Christ, he must needs have charity; for if he have not charity he is nothing; wherefore he must needs have charity."[3]

Looking back, I now see how that gift of charity—the pure love of Christ—strengthened, guided, sustained, and changed my mother in the struggle on her way home.

"And charity suffereth long, and is kind, and envieth not, and is not puffed up, seeketh not her own, is not easily provoked, thinketh no evil, and rejoiceth not in iniquity but rejoiceth in the truth, beareth all things, believeth all things, hopeth all things, endureth all things.

"Wherefore, my beloved brethren, if ye have not charity, ye are nothing, for charity never faileth. Wherefore, cleave unto charity, which is the greatest of all, for all things must fail—

"But charity is the pure love of Christ, and it endureth forever; and whoso is found possessed of it at the last day, it shall be well with him.

"Wherefore, my beloved brethren, pray unto the Father with all the energy of heart, that ye may be filled with this love, which he hath bestowed upon all who are true followers of his Son, Jesus Christ; that ye may become the sons of God; that when he shall appear we shall be like him, for we shall see him as he is; that we may have this hope; that we may be purified even as he is pure."[4]

I am grateful for the encouragement of Mormon's example and teaching. I have been blessed as well by my mother's legacy. Prophets from Adam to the present day, through teaching and by example, have strengthened me.

Out of deference to those I know personally and their families, I have chosen not to seek to verify the details of their struggles or to speak of their great gifts publicly. Yet what I have seen has encouraged me and changed me for the better.

At the risk of invading her privacy, I will add a brief report of the encouragement of my wife. I do so carefully. She is a private person who neither seeks nor appreciates praise.

We have been married for 60 years. It is because of that experience that I now understand the meaning of these scriptural words: faith, hope, meekness, enduring, seeking not our own, rejoicing in the truth, not thinking evil, and above all, charity.[5] On the basis of that experience, I can bear testimony that apparently ordinary human beings can take all of those wonderful ideals into their daily lives as they rise through the buffetings of life.

Millions of you listening know such people. Many of you *are* such people. All of us need such encouraging examples and loving friends.

When you sit with someone as their ministering sister or brother, you represent the Lord. Think of what He would do or say. He would invite them to come unto Him. He would encourage them. He would notice and praise the beginning of the changes they will need to make. And He would be the perfect example for them to emulate.

No one can completely do that yet, but by listening to this conference, you can know you are on the way. The Savior knows your struggles in detail. He knows your great potential to grow in faith, hope, and charity.

The commandments and covenants He offers you are not tests to control you. They are a gift to lift you toward receiving all the gifts of God and returning home to your Heavenly Father and the Lord, who love you.

Jesus Christ paid the price of our sins. We may claim that blessing of eternal life if we will have faith in Him enough to repent and become like a child, pure and ready to receive the greatest of all the gifts of God.

I pray that you will accept His invitation and that you will offer it to others of our Heavenly Father's children.

I pray for our missionaries across the world. May they be inspired to encourage each person to want and to believe that the invitation is from Jesus Christ through His servants who have taken His name upon them.

I testify that He lives and leads His Church. I am His witness.

President Russell M. Nelson is the living prophet of God for all the earth. I know that is true. In the sacred name of Jesus Christ, amen.

Notes

1. Moroni 7:38–39.
2. Moroni 7:40–43.
3. Moroni 7:44.
4. Moroni 7:45–48.
5. See 1 Corinthians 13; Moroni 7.

THE ANSWER IS JESUS

ELDER RYAN K. OLSEN
Of the Seventy

What an honor to speak to you in this session of conference. Today I address you as friends. In the Gospel of John, the Savior taught that we are His friends if we do what He asks us to do.[1]

It is our individual and collective love of the Savior, and our covenants with Him, that bind us together. As President Henry B. Eyring taught: "To you I wish to say how much the Lord loves you and trusts you. And, even more, I wish to tell you how much He depends on you."[2]

When I was called as a General Authority by President Russell M. Nelson, I was flooded with emotions. It was overwhelming. My wife, Julie, and I anxiously awaited the Saturday afternoon session of general conference. It was humbling to be sustained. I carefully counted the steps to my designated seat so as not to fall in my first assignment.

At the conclusion of that session, something happened that had a profound effect on me. The quorum members formed a line and greeted the new General Authorities one by one. Each one shared their love and support. With a hearty *abrazo* they said, "Don't worry—you belong."

In our relationship with the Savior, He looks on the heart and is "no respecter of persons."[3] Consider how He chose His Apostles. He didn't pay attention to status or wealth. He invites us to follow Him, and I believe He reassures us that we belong with Him.

This message especially applies to the youth of the Church. I see in you what President Nelson sees in you. He said that "there is something undeniably special about this generation of youth. Your Heavenly Father must have great confidence in you to send you to earth at this time. You were born for greatness!"[4]

I am grateful for what I learn from the youth. I am grateful for what my children teach me, for what our missionaries teach me, and for what my nieces and nephews teach me.

Not too long ago, I was working on our farm with my nephew

Nash. He is six and has a pure heart. He is my favorite nephew named Nash, and I believe I am his favorite uncle speaking in conference today.

As he helped me come up with a solution for our project, I said, "Nash, that is a great idea. How did you get so smart?" He looked at me with an expression in his eyes that said, "Uncle Ryan, how do you not know the answer to this question?"

He simply shrugged his shoulders, smiled, and confidently said, "Jesus."

Nash reminded me that day of this simple and yet profound teaching. The answer to the simplest questions and to the most complex problems is always the same. The answer is Jesus Christ. Every solution is found in Him.

In the Gospel of John, the Savior said to His disciples that He would prepare a place for them. Thomas was confused and said to the Savior:

"Lord, we know not whither thou goest; and how can we know the way?

"Jesus saith unto him, I am the way, the truth, and the life: no man cometh unto the Father, but by me."[5]

The Savior taught His disciples that He is "the way, the truth, and the life." He is the answer to the question of how to come unto Heavenly Father. Gaining a testimony of His divine role in our lives was something I learned as a young man.

While I was serving as a missionary in Argentina, President Howard W. Hunter invited us to do something that had a profound effect on my life. He said, "We must know Christ better than we know him; we must remember him more often than we remember him; we must serve him more valiantly than we serve him."[6]

At that time, I had been concerned with how to be a better missionary. This was the answer: to know Christ, to remember Him, and to serve Him. Missionaries throughout the world are united in this purpose: to "invite others to come unto Christ by helping them receive the restored gospel through faith in [Him] and His Atonement" and through "repentance, baptism, receiving the gift of the Holy Ghost, and enduring to the end."[7] To our friends who are listening to the missionaries, I add my invitation to come unto Christ. Together we will strive to know Him, remember Him, and serve Him.

Serving a mission was a sacred time of my life. In my last interview with him as a full-time missionary, President Blair Pincock spoke of the upcoming change in mission leaders, as he and his wife were also nearing the completion of their service. We were both sad to be leaving something we loved so much. He could see that I was troubled by the thought of not being a full-time missionary. He was a man of great faith and lovingly taught me as he had for the previous two years. He pointed to the picture of Jesus Christ above his desk and said, "Elder Olsen, it is all going to be OK because it is His work." I felt reassured knowing that the Savior will help us, not just while we are serving but always—if we will let Him.

Sister Pincock taught us from the depths of her heart in the simplest Spanish phrases. When she said, "Jesucristo vive," I knew it was true and that He lived. When she said, "Elderes y hermanas, les amo," I knew that she loved us and wanted us to follow the Savior always.

My wife and I were recently blessed to serve as mission leaders to labor with the outstanding missionaries in Uruguay. I would say that these were the best missionaries in the world, and I trust that every mission leader feels that way. These disciples taught us every day about following the Savior.

During regular interviews one of our great sister missionaries walked into the office. She was a successful missionary, an excellent trainer, and a dedicated leader. She was looked up to by her companions and loved by the people. She was obedient, humble, and confident. Our previous visits focused on her area and the people she was teaching. This visit was different. As I asked her how she was doing, I could tell she was troubled. She said, "President Olsen, I don't know if I can do this. I don't know if I will ever be good enough. I don't know if I can be the missionary that the Lord needs me to be."

She was a remarkable missionary. Excellent in every way. A mission president's dream. I had never worried about her abilities as a missionary.

As I listened to her, I struggled to know what to say. I silently prayed: "Heavenly Father, this is an outstanding missionary. She is Yours. She is doing everything right. I don't want to mess this up. Please help me know what to say."

The words came to me. I said, "*Hermana*, I am so sorry you are feeling this way. Let me ask you a question. If you had a friend you were teaching who felt this way, what would you say?"

She looked at me and smiled. With that unmistakable missionary spirit and conviction, she said, "President, that is easy. I would tell her that the Savior knows her perfectly. I would tell her that He lives. He loves you. You are good enough, and you've got this!"

With a little chuckle she said, "I guess if that applies to our friends, then it also applies to me."

When we have questions or doubts, we may feel that the solutions are too complex or that finding answers is too confusing. May we remember that the adversary, even the father of all lies, is the architect of confusion.[8]

The Savior is the Master of simplicity.

President Nelson has said:

"The adversary is clever. For millennia he has been making good look evil and evil look good. His messages tend to be loud, bold, and boastful.

"However, messages from our Heavenly Father are strikingly different. He communicates simply, quietly, and with such stunning plainness that we cannot misunderstand Him."[9]

How grateful we are that God so loved us that He sent His Son. He is the answer.

President Nelson recently said:

"The gospel of Jesus Christ has never been needed more than it is today. . . .

". . . This underscores the urgent need for us to follow the Lord's instruction to His disciples to 'go . . . into *all* the world, and preach the gospel to *every* creature.'"[10]

To those who will choose to serve, I can attest to the blessings that will come as you heed a prophet's call. Serving is not about you; it is about the Savior. You will be called to a place, but more importantly you will be called to a people. You will have the great responsibility and blessing of helping new friends understand that the answer is Jesus.

This is The Church of Jesus Christ of Latter-day Saints, and this is where we belong. Everything that President Nelson lovingly encourages us to do will lead us closer to the Savior.

To our magnificent youth—including my nephew Nash— throughout your life, no matter how difficult or confusing the challenges may be, you can always remember that the answer is simple: it is always Jesus.

As I have heard those who we sustain as prophets, seers, and revelators say on many occasions, I also say that we love you, we thank you, and we need you. This is where you belong.

I love the Savior. I bear witness of His name, even Jesus Christ. I testify that He is "the author and finisher of our faith,"[11] and He is the Master of simplicity. The answer is Jesus. In the name of Jesus Christ, amen.

Notes

1. See John 15:14.
2. Henry B. Eyring, "Hearts Bound Together," *Ensign* or *Liahona*, May 2005, 77.
3. See 1 Samuel 16:7; Acts 10:34–35; Doctrine and Covenants 1:34–35.
4. Russell M. Nelson, in "Worldwide Youth Devotional: Messages from President Russell M. Nelson and Sister Wendy W. Nelson," June 3, 2018, ChurchofJesusChrist.org.
5. John 14:5–6.
6. Howard W. Hunter, "What Manner of Men Ought Ye to Be?," *Ensign*, May 1994, 64.
7. *Preach My Gospel: A Guide to Missionary Service* (2019), 1.
8. See 1 Corinthians 14:33; James 3:16; Doctrine and Covenants 123:7; 132:8.
9. Russell M. Nelson, "Hear Him," *Ensign* or *Liahona*, May 2020, 89.
10. Russell M. Nelson, "Preaching the Gospel of Peace," *Liahona*, May 2022, 6.
11. Hebrews 12:2.

THAT THEY MIGHT KNOW THEE (JOHN 17:3)

ELDER JONATHAN S. SCHMITT
Of the Seventy

A few years ago, I had a life-changing experience during a sacrament meeting in our home ward in Arizona. As the sacrament prayer indicated our willingness to "take upon [ourselves] the name of [Jesus Christ],"[1] the Holy Ghost reminded me that Jesus has many names. This question then came to my heart: "Which of Jesus's names should I take upon myself this week?"

Three names came to my mind, and I wrote them down. Each of those three names contained Christlike attributes that I wanted to develop more fully. In the week that followed, I focused on those three names and tried to embrace their corresponding attributes and characteristics. Since that time, I've continued to ask that question as part of my personal worship: "Which of Jesus's names should I take upon myself this week?" Answering that question and striving to develop the related Christlike attributes has blessed my life.

In His great Intercessory Prayer, Jesus expressed this important truth: "And this is life eternal, that *they might know thee* the only true God, and Jesus Christ, whom thou hast sent."[2] Today I'd like to share with you the blessings and power that come from knowing Jesus Christ by His many names.

One simple way we get to know someone is by learning their name. It has been said that "a person's name is to that person the sweetest and most important sound in any language."[3] Have you ever had the experience of calling someone by the wrong name or forgetting their name? My wife, Alexis, and I have, on occasion, called one of our children "Lola." Unfortunately, as you may have guessed, Lola is our dog! For better or worse, forgetting someone's name communicates to that person that you probably don't know them very well.

Jesus knew and called people by name. To ancient Israel, the Lord said, "Fear not: for I have redeemed thee, *I have called thee by thy name*; thou art mine."[4] On Easter morning, Mary's witness of the resurrected Christ was solidified when Jesus called her by name.[5] Likewise, God called Joseph Smith by name in answer to his prayer of faith.[6]

In some cases, Jesus gave His disciples new names that were indicative of their nature, capacity, and potential. Jehovah gave Jacob the new name of Israel, which means "one who prevails with God" or "let God prevail."[7] Jesus gave James and John the name of Boanerges, which meant the "sons of thunder."[8] Seeing his future leadership, Jesus gave Simon the name of Cephas or Peter, which means a rock.[9]

Just as Jesus knows each of us by name, one way we can come to better know Jesus is by learning His many names. Like the names of Israel and Peter, many of Jesus's names are titles that help us understand His mission, purpose, character, and attributes. As we come to know Jesus's many names, we will come to better understand His divine mission and His selfless character. Knowing His many names also inspires us to become more like Him—to develop Christlike attributes that bring joy and purpose to our lives.

A few years ago, President Russell M. Nelson studied all the scriptures concerning Jesus Christ in the Topical Guide.[10] He then invited young adults to study these same scriptures. Concerning Jesus's many names, President Nelson said, "Study everything Jesus Christ *is* by prayerfully and vigorously seeking to understand what each of His various titles and names means *personally* for you."[11]

Following President Nelson's invitation, I began developing my own list of Jesus's many names. My personal list now has over 300 names, and I'm sure there are many more that I haven't discovered yet.

While there are some of Jesus's names that are reserved only for Him,[12] I would like to share five names and titles that have application to each of us. I invite you to develop your own list as you come to know Jesus by His many names. In doing so, you will find that there are other names—along with their corresponding Christlike attributes—that you will want to take upon yourself as Jesus's covenant disciple.[13]

First, Jesus is the **Good Shepherd**.[14] As such, Jesus knows His sheep,[15] "calleth his own sheep by name,"[16] and, as the Lamb of God, gave His life for His sheep.[17] Similarly, Jesus wants us to be good shepherds, particularly in our families and as ministering brothers and sisters. One way we demonstrate our love for Jesus is by feeding His sheep.[18] For those sheep who may be wandering, good shepherds go into the wilderness to find the lost sheep and then stay with them until they return to safety.[19] As good shepherds and as local conditions permit, we should seek to spend more time ministering to people in their homes. In our ministering, texting and technology should be used to enhance, not replace, personal contact.[20]

Second, Jesus is the **High Priest of Good Things to Come**.[21] Knowing that His Crucifixion was just hours away, Jesus said: "These things I have spoken unto you, that in me ye might have peace. In the world ye shall have tribulation: but be of good cheer; I have overcome the world."[22] Today, as our world is frequently polarized and divided, there is a great need for us to preach and practice positivity, optimism, and hope. Despite any challenges in our past, faith always points toward the future,[23] filled with hope, allowing us to fulfill Jesus's invitation to be of good cheer.[24] Joyfully living the gospel helps us to become *disciples of good things to come*.

Another of Jesus's titles is that He is **the Same, Yesterday, Today, and Forever**.[25] Consistency is a Christlike attribute. Jesus always did His Father's will,[26] and His arm is constantly outstretched to save, help, and heal us.[27] As we are more consistent in living the gospel, we will become more like Jesus.[28] Although the world will experience large swings in its pendulums of popularity as people are tossed to and fro and carried about with every wind of doctrine,[29] consistent gospel living helps us to be steadfast and immovable during the storms of life.[30] We can also demonstrate consistency by accepting President Nelson's invitation to "make time for the Lord."[31] Great spiritual strength comes from small and simple things[32] like developing "holy habits and righteous routines"[33] of daily prayer, repentance, scripture study, and service to others.

Fourth, Jesus is the **Holy One of Israel**.[34] Jesus's life was a pattern of holiness. As we follow Jesus, we can become a holy one *in*

Israel.[35] We increase in holiness as we regularly visit the temple, where "Holiness to the Lord" is etched above every entrance. Every time we worship in the temple, we leave endowed with greater power to make our homes places of holiness.[36] For any who do not currently have a recommend to enter the holy temple, I invite you to meet with your bishop and prepare yourself to enter or return to that holy place. Time in the temple will increase holiness in our lives.

One last name of Jesus is that He is **Faithful and True**.[37] Just as Jesus was ever faithful and always true, His earnest desire is that we exhibit these qualities in our lives. When our faith falters, we can cry out to Jesus, "Lord, save me," just like Peter as he began to sink in Galilee's stormy sea.[38] On that day, Jesus reached down to rescue the drowning disciple. He has done the same for me, and He will do the same for you. Don't ever give up on Jesus—He will never give up on you!

When we are faithful and true, we follow Jesus's call to "abide in me," which can also mean "stay with me."[39] When we are confronted with questions, when we are mocked for our faith, when the fingers of scorn are pointed at us by those in the world's great and spacious buildings, we remain faithful and we stay true. In these moments, we remember Jesus's plea: "Look unto me in every thought; doubt not, fear not."[40] As we do so, He gives us needed faith, hope, and strength to stay with Him forever.[41]

Dear brothers and sisters, Jesus wants for us to know Him because His is the only name under heaven whereby we can be saved.[42] Jesus is the Way, the Truth, and the Life—no one can return to the Father except by Him.[43] Jesus is the only way! For that reason, Jesus beckons, "Come unto me,"[44] "Follow me,"[45] "Walk with me,"[46] and "Learn of me."[47]

With all my heart, I bear witness of Jesus Christ—that He lives, that He loves you, and that He knows you by name. He is the Son of God,[48] the Only Begotten of the Father.[49] He is our Rock, our Fortress, our Shield, our Refuge, and our Deliverer.[50] He is the Light which Shineth in Darkness.[51] He is our Savior[52] and our Redeemer.[53] He is the Resurrection and the Life.[54] My earnest desire is that you will come to know Jesus by His many names and that you will become like Him as you exemplify His divine attributes in your life. In the name of Jesus Christ, amen.

Notes

1. Doctrine and Covenants 20:77.
2. John 17:3; emphasis added. Concerning this prayer, President David O. McKay taught: "This text is taken from one of the most glorious prayers—I suppose the greatest prayer—ever uttered in this world, not excepting the Lord's Prayer. This was Christ's prayer uttered just before he entered the Garden of Gethsemane on the night of his betrayal. . . . I know of no more important chapter in the Bible" (in Conference Report, Oct. 1967, 5).
3. Dale Carnegie, *How to Win Friends and Influence People*, rev. ed. (1981), 83.
4. Isaiah 43:1; emphasis added.
5. See John 20:16.
6. See Joseph Smith—History 1:17.
7. Bible Dictionary, "Israel."
8. Mark 3:17.
9. See Luke 6:14; John 1:42.
10. See Russell M. Nelson, "I Studied More Than 2,200 Scriptures about the Savior in Six Weeks: Here Is a Little of What I Learned," *Inspiration* (blog), Feb. 28, 2017, ChurchofJesusChrist.org. Following this experience, President Nelson exclaimed, "I am a different man!" ("Drawing the Power of Jesus Christ into Our Lives," *Ensign* or *Liahona*, May 2017, 39).
11. Russell M. Nelson, "Prophets, Leadership, and Divine Law" (worldwide devotional for young adults, Jan. 8, 2017), broadcasts.ChurchofJesusChrist.org.
12. For example, Jesus is Messiah, the Christ, Great Jehovah, the Firstborn from the Dead, and the Only Begotten Son of God.
13. In addition to President Nelson's invitation to study the scriptures concerning Jesus in the Topical Guide, you can also study Jesus's many names by referring to the Bible Dictionary under "Christ, names of." You may also wish to study Elder Jeffrey R. Holland's book *Witness for His Names* (2019) and a devotional talk by Elder Ronald A. Rasband titled "Name above All Names" (Brigham Young University–Hawaii devotional, Oct. 20, 2020), speeches.byuh.edu.
14. See John 10:11.
15. See John 10:14.
16. John 10:3.
17. See John 10:11–15; 1 Nephi 11:31–33.
18. See John 21:15–17.
19. I particularly like the Joseph Smith Translation of Luke 15:4, which reads, "What man of you, having an hundred sheep, if he lose one of them, doth not leave the ninety and nine *and go into the wilderness after that which is lost*, until he find it?" (in Luke 15:4, footnote *a*; emphasis added).
20. As Elder David A. Bednar observed: "Everybody thinks a text is enough [for ministering]. There are occasions where you need to be in the home and you need to look the people in the eyes, because you're going to receive impressions and inspiration in the home that you'll never get any other way" ("An Evening with Elder David A. Bednar" [broadcast for religious educators], Feb. 7, 2020], broadcasts.ChurchofJesusChrist.org).
21. See Hebrews 9:11.
22. John 16:33.
23. See Jeffrey R. Holland, "'Remember Lot's Wife': Faith Is for the Future" (Brigham Young University devotional, Jan. 13, 2009), 2, speeches.byu.edu. *Faith is always pointed toward the future. Faith always has to do with blessings and truths and events that will *yet* be efficacious in our lives."
24. See Matthew 9:2; Mark 6:50; John 16:33; 3 Nephi 1:13; Doctrine and Covenants 61:36.
25. See Hebrews 13:8; see also Bible Dictionary, "Christ, names of."
26. See John 8:29.
27. See Alma 5:33; 19:36; 3 Nephi 9:14.

28. See, for example, David A. Bednar, "More Diligent and Concerned at Home," *Ensign* or *Liahona*, Nov. 2009, 20: "Consistency is a key principle as we lay the foundation of a great work in our individual lives. . . . We need to be and become more consistent."
29. See Ephesians 4:14.
30. See Mosiah 5:15.
31. Russell M. Nelson, "Make Time for the Lord," *Liahona*, Nov. 2021, 120.
32. See Alma 37:6.
33. This is a phrase that President Dallin H. Oaks has repeated several times in his ministry. See, for example, "YSA Face to Face with Elder Oaks and Elder Ballard" (broadcast for young single adults, Nov. 19, 2017), ChurchofJesusChrist.org.
34. See 2 Nephi 9:18–19, 41.
35. In a recent worldwide devotional for young adults, Sister Wendy Nelson posed a question that she said could change lives, increase confidence and decrease anxiety, motivate, increase gratitude and decrease stress, help resist temptation, and bring joy, comfort, love, and peace. That question was "What would a holy young adult do?" She then encouraged application of this question in just one situation each day for three successive days. See "One Question That Can Change Your Life" (worldwide devotional for young adults, May 15, 2022), broadcasts.ChurchofJesusChrist.org.
36. See Doctrine and Covenants 109:12–13, 22.
37. See Revelation 19:11.
38. Matthew 14:30.
39. John 15:4. The Greek word for *abide* is μείνατε (meinate or menó), which means to stay or remain.
40. Doctrine and Covenants 6:36.
41. Elder Jeffrey R. Holland once noted that, in Spanish, the English phrase "abide in me" is translated as "permaneced en mi." He continued: "The sense of this then is 'stay—but stay *forever.*' . . . Come permanently, for your sake and the sake of all the generations who must follow you, and we will help each other be strong to the very end" ("Abide in Me," *Ensign* or *Liahona*, May 2004, 32).
42. See 2 Nephi 31:21.
43. See John 14:6.
44. Matthew 11:28; 3 Nephi 9:14, 22.
45. Matthew 16:24; Luke 18:22; John 21:19; see also 2 Nephi 31:10.
46. Revelation 3:4; Moses 6:34.
47. Matthew 11:29; Doctrine and Covenants 19:23.
48. See 3 Nephi 9:15.
49. See John 1:14; Alma 5:48.
50. See 2 Samuel 22:2–3.
51. See Doctrine and Covenants 6:21.
52. See Luke 2:11.
53. See Doctrine and Covenants 18:11–13.
54. See John 11:25.

THE VIRTUE OF THE WORD

ELDER MARK D. EDDY
Of the Seventy

In the Book of Mormon, we read of a vital decision made by the prophet Alma in a beloved verse of scripture. Prior to reviewing those familiar words, please consider with me the difficult circumstances under which that decision was made.

A faction of people, calling themselves Zoramites, had separated from the Nephites[1] and gathered in the borders of the land near the Lamanites.[2] The Nephites had recently defeated the Lamanites in an unprecedented battle in which tens of thousands were killed,[3] and it was "greatly feared that the Zoramites would enter into a correspondence with the Lamanites, and that it would be the means of great loss."[4] Beyond the concerns of war, Alma had learned that the Zoramites, who "had had the word of God preached unto them,"[5] were turning to idol worship and "perverting the ways of the Lord."[6] All of this weighed heavily on Alma and was "the cause of great sorrow."[7]

Finding himself in these complex and challenging circumstances, Alma pondered what should be done. In his decision we read words that were preserved to inspire and instruct us as we navigate the complex and challenging circumstances of our day.[8]

"And now, as the preaching of the word had a great tendency to lead the people to do that which was just—yea, it had had more powerful effect upon the minds of the people than the sword, or anything else, which had happened unto them—therefore Alma thought it was expedient that they should *try the virtue of the word of God.*"[9]

Among many possible solutions, Alma's faith led them to rely on the power of the word. It is no coincidence that some of the most powerful sermons found anywhere in scripture were preached immediately following that decision. In chapters 32 and 33 of Alma, we read his masterful discourse on faith in the Lord Jesus Christ, and in chapter 34 we find Amulek's seminal teachings on the Atonement of Jesus Christ.

Illustrations of the Virtue of the Word

Indeed, throughout scripture we read of miraculous blessings poured out upon those who have chosen to try the virtue of the word of God in their lives.[10] I invite you to ponder three examples with me as we turn our focus to the Book of Mormon—a book that President Russell M. Nelson described as "our *latter-day* survival guide."[11]

First, reminding his people how the Lord delivered their fathers, Alma taught: "Behold, he changed their hearts; yea, he awakened them out of a deep sleep, and they awoke unto God. Behold, they were in the midst of darkness; nevertheless, *their souls were illuminated by the light of the everlasting word.*"[12] Perhaps you are feeling as though you were in the midst of darkness. Does your soul ache for illumination? If so, please try the virtue of the word of God.

Second, reflecting on the Lord's conversion of the Lamanites, which he witnessed as a missionary, Ammon said, "Behold, how many thousands of our brethren has he loosed from the pains of hell; and they are brought to sing redeeming love, and *this because of the power of his word which is in us.*"[13] Brothers and sisters, there are so many among us who are yearning for someone we love to be brought to sing redeeming love. In all our efforts, let us remember to try the virtue of the word of God, which is in us.

Third, in the book of Helaman we read, "Yea, we see that whosoever *will* may lay hold upon *the word of God, which is quick and powerful,* which shall divide asunder all the cunning and the snares and the wiles of the devil, and lead the man [and woman] of Christ in a strait and narrow course across that everlasting gulf of misery . . . and land their souls . . . at the right hand of God in the kingdom of heaven."[14] Are you seeking to cut through all the cunning and the snares and the wiles of the devil so prevalent in the philosophies of our day? Do you desire to disperse the clouds of confusion caused by an overabundance of information in order to focus more singularly on the covenant path? Please try the virtue of the word of God.

As one who has been changed by the power of the word, I personally testify of this truth so beautifully taught by our beloved prophet, President Russell M. Nelson: "To me, the power of the Book of Mormon is most evident in the mighty change that comes into the lives of those who read it 'with a sincere heart, with real intent, having faith in Christ.' Many converts forsake much that they once held dear in order to abide by the precepts of that book. . . . It will be your most effective instrument in bringing souls unto Jesus the Christ."[15]

The Source of Virtue

In these and other illustrations, we witness the virtue of the word of God in the lives of His children. We might ask, what is the source of that virtue or power?

As we consider this question, it is essential to remember that the phrase "the word," as used in scripture, has at least two meanings. Elder David A. Bednar recently taught that "one of the names of Jesus Christ is 'The Word'" and that "the teachings of the Savior, as recorded in the holy scriptures, also are 'the word.'"[16]

The prophet Nephi illustrated the relationship between these two meanings when he wrote: "Hearken unto these words and believe in Christ; and if ye believe not in these words believe in Christ. And if ye shall believe in Christ ye *will* believe in these words, for they are the words of Christ, and he hath given them unto me."[17] Thus we learn that there is virtue in the words of ancient and modern prophets *precisely* because their words are the Lord's words.[18] My dear friends, accepting this eternal truth is critical to our spiritual survival in the latter days[19] when, as prophesied, there is "a famine in the land, not a famine of bread, nor a thirst for water, but of hearing the words of the Lord."[20]

Ultimately, the virtue of the word of God *is* the Lord Jesus Christ.[21] As we comprehend this more fully, we can make an eternally significant connection between the role of His prophets and the Redeemer Himself. Our love for Him, our desire to draw closer to Him and to abide in His love,[22] will motivate us to try the virtue of the word in our lives—both the virtue that flows from Him as our personal Savior and Redeemer[23] and the virtue that flows from Him through the words of "the chosen vessels of the Lord."[24] We will come to discern that, as helpful as other sources may be in our study of the Savior and the words of His prophets, they must never become a replacement for them. We must drink deeply and often[25] directly from the source.[26]

I express my love to each of you, my brothers and my sisters. In that love, I plead with you to experience the virtue of the word of God, particularly through the Book of Mormon, every day of your life. As you do so, you will experience this prophetic promise from President Russell M. Nelson: "I promise that as you prayerfully study the Book of Mormon *every day*, you will make better decisions—*every day*. I promise that as you ponder what you study, the windows of heaven will open, and you will receive answers to your own questions and direction for your own life. I promise that as you daily immerse yourself in the Book of Mormon, you can be immunized against the evils of the day."[27]

I testify that our Heavenly Father has given us the word because He loves us perfectly and wants each of us to return home to live with Him forever. I testify of "the Word . . . made flesh,"[28] even Jesus the Christ, and of His power to save and to redeem us. I know that His virtue flows through the words of His prophets, both past and present.

It is the prayer of my heart that we may possess the wisdom and meekness to hold fast[29] to the word of God and stay on the covenant path that leads to exaltation and eternal life.[30] May we continually experience the mighty change available to each of us through the virtue of the Word.[31] In the name of Jesus Christ, amen.

Notes

1. See Alma 30:59.
2. See Alma 31:3.
3. See Alma 28:2.
4. Alma 31:4. Please note that Alma and his people previously experienced such a "correspondence"

between the Amlicites and Lamanites, which led to great sorrow and loss (see Alma 2:21–38; 3:1–3).

5. Alma 31:8.
6. Alma 31:1.
7. Alma 31:2.
8. See Mormon 8:34–35.
9. Alma 31:5; emphasis added.
10. See, for example, 1 Nephi 15:24; Alma 32:41–43; 36:26; 37:8, 44–45.
11. Russell M. Nelson, "Embrace the Future with Faith," *Ensign* or *Liahona*, Nov. 2020, 75.
12. Alma 5:7; emphasis added.
13. Alma 26:13; emphasis added.
14. Helaman 3:29–30; emphasis added.
15. Russell M. Nelson, "The Book of Mormon: A Miraculous Miracle" (address given at the seminar for new mission leaders, June 23, 2016), quoting in part Moroni 10:4.
16. David A. Bednar, "But We Heeded Them Not," *Liahona*, May 2022, 16.
17. 2 Nephi 33:10; emphasis added.
18. See Doctrine and Covenants 1:38.
19. See Doctrine and Covenants 1:14–18.
20. Amos 8:11.
21. See Alma 34:6.
22. See John 15:10.
23. See Mark 5:25–34.
24. Moroni 7:31.
25. "There is a better way to prepare, because great faith has a short shelf life. We could decide to persist in studying the words of Christ in the scriptures and the teachings of living prophets. This is what I will do. I will go back to the Book of Mormon and drink deeply and often" (Henry B. Eyring, "Spiritual Preparedness: Start Early and Be Steady," *Ensign* or *Liahona*, Nov. 2005, 39).
26. "For me, the reading of the scriptures is not the pursuit of scholarship. Rather, it is a love affair with the word of the Lord and that of his prophets. . . .

    "I do not concern myself much with reading long commentary volumes designed to enlarge at length upon that which is found in the scriptures. Rather, I prefer to dwell with the source, tasting of the unadulterated waters of the foundation of truth—the word of God as he gave it and as it has been recorded in the books we accept as scripture. Through reading the scriptures, we can gain the assurance of the Spirit that that which we read has come of God for the enlightenment, blessing, and joy of his children" (Gordon B. Hinckley, "Feasting upon the Scriptures," *Ensign*, Dec. 1985, 44, 45; *Tambuli*, June 1986, 2, 4).
27. Russell M. Nelson, "The Book of Mormon: What Would Your Life Be Like without It?," *Ensign* or *Liahona*, Nov. 2017, 62–63.
28. John 1:14.
29. See 1 Nephi 8:30.
30. "The covenant path is the *only* path that leads to exaltation and eternal life" (Russell M. Nelson, "The Power of Spiritual Momentum," *Liahona*, May 2022, 98).
31. See Alma 5:11–13.

NOURISHING AND BEARING YOUR TESTIMONY

ELDER GARY E. STEVENSON
Of the Quorum of the Twelve Apostles

Introduction

Defining moments in life come often and unexpectedly, even when you are still young. Allow me to share a story about a high school student, Kevin, chosen to travel out of state for a student leader event, as told in his own words.

"My turn in line came, and the official-looking registration clerk asked for my name. She looked at her list and said, 'So you're the young man from Utah.'

"'You mean I'm the only one?' I asked.

"'Yes, the only one.' She handed me my name tag with 'Utah' printed below my name. As I clipped it on, I felt like I was being branded.

"I crowded into the hotel elevator with five other high school students with name tags like mine. 'Hey, you're from Utah. Are you a Mormon?' asked one student.

"I felt out of place with all these student leaders from all over the country. 'Yes,' I hesitantly admitted.

"'You're the guys who believe in Joseph Smith, who said he saw angels. You don't actually believe that, do you?'

"I didn't know what to say. The students in the elevator were all staring at me. I had just arrived, and already everyone thought I was different. I became a little defensive but then said, 'I know that Joseph Smith was a prophet of God.'

"'Where had that come from?' I wondered. I didn't know I had it in me. But the words felt true.

"'Yeah, I was told that you were all just religious nuts,' he said.

"With that, there was an uncomfortable pause as the elevator door opened. As we gathered our luggage, he walked down the hall laughing.

"Then, a voice behind me asked, 'Hey, don't Mormons have some sort of another Bible?'

"Oh no. Not again. I turned to see another student who had been in the elevator with me, Christopher.

"'It's called the Book of Mormon,' I said, wanting to drop the subject. I picked up my bags and started walking down the hall.

"'Is that the book Joseph Smith translated?' he asked.

"'Yeah, it is,' I answered. I kept on walking, hoping to avoid embarrassment.

"'Well, do you know how I could get one?'

"A scripture I learned in seminary suddenly came to me. 'I am not ashamed of the gospel of Jesus Christ.'[1] As this entered my mind, I felt ashamed I had been so embarrassed.

"For the rest of the week that scripture wouldn't leave me. I answered as many questions about the Church as I could, and I made many friends.

"I discovered I was proud of my religion.

"I gave Christopher a Book of Mormon. He later wrote me, telling me he had invited the missionaries to his home.

"I learned not to be embarrassed to share my testimony."[2]

I am inspired by Kevin's courage in sharing his testimony. It is a courage repeated every day by faithful members of the Church throughout the world. As I share my thoughts, I invite you to reflect upon these four questions:

1. Do I know and understand what a testimony is?
2. Do I know how to bear my testimony?
3. What are the obstacles in sharing my testimony?
4. How do I keep my testimony?

Do I Know and Understand What a Testimony Is?

Your testimony is a most precious possession, often associated with deep spiritual feelings. These feelings are usually communicated quietly and described as a "still small voice."[3] It is your belief or knowledge of truth given as a spiritual witness through the influence of the Holy Ghost. Acquiring this witness will change what you say and how you act. Key elements of your testimony, confirmed by the Holy Ghost, include:

- God is your Heavenly Father; you are His child. He loves you.
- Jesus Christ lives. He is the Son of the living God and your Savior and Redeemer.
- Joseph Smith is a prophet of God called to restore the Church of Jesus Christ.
- The Church of Jesus Christ of Latter-day Saints is God's restored Church on the earth.
- The restored Church of Jesus Christ is led by a living prophet today.

Do I Know How to Bear My Testimony?

You bear your testimony when you share spiritual feelings with others. As a member of the Church, you have opportunities to bear your spoken testimony in formal Church meetings or in less formal, one-on-one conversations with family, friends, and others.

Another way you share your testimony is through righteous behavior. Your testimony in Jesus Christ isn't just what you say—it's who you are.

Each time you bear vocal witness or demonstrate through your actions your commitment to follow Jesus Christ, you invite others to "come unto Christ."[4]

Members of the Church stand as witnesses of God at all times, in all things, and in all places.[5] Opportunities to do this in the digital universe using inspiring content of our own or sharing uplifting content prepared by others are endless. We testify when we love, share, and invite, even online. Your tweets, direct messages, and posts will take on a higher, holier purpose when you also use social media to show how the gospel of Jesus Christ shapes your life.

What Are the Obstacles in Sharing My Testimony?

Obstacles to sharing your testimony may include uncertainty about what to say. Matthew Cowley, an early Apostle, shared this experience as he departed on a five-year mission at age 17 to New Zealand:

"I will never forget the prayers of my father the day that I left. I have never heard a more beautiful blessing in all my life. Then his last words to me at the railroad station, 'My boy, you will go out on that mission; you will study; you will try to prepare your sermons; and sometimes when you are called upon, you will think you are wonderfully prepared, but when you stand up, your mind will go completely blank.' I have had that experience more than once.

"I said, 'What do you do when your mind goes blank?'

"He said, 'You stand up there and with all the fervor of your soul, you bear witness that Joseph Smith was a prophet of the living God, and thoughts will flood into your mind and words to your mouth . . . to the heart of everyone who listens.' And so my mind, being mostly blank during my . . . mission . . . , gave me the opportunity to bear testimony to the greatest event in the history of the world since the crucifixion of the Master. Try it sometime, fellows and girls. If you don't have anything else to say, testify that Joseph Smith was the prophet of God, and the whole history of the Church will flood into your mind."[6]

Likewise, President Dallin H. Oaks shared, "Some testimonies are better gained on the feet bearing them than on the knees praying for them."[7] The Spirit bears witness to the speaker and listener alike.

Another obstacle, as Kevin's story emphasized, is fear. As Paul wrote to Timothy:

"God hath not given us the spirit of fear; but of power, and of love. . . .

"Be not thou therefore ashamed of the testimony of our Lord."[8]

Feelings of fear don't come from the Lord but most often from the adversary. Having faith, as Kevin did, will allow you to overcome these feelings and freely share what is in your heart.

How Do I Keep My Testimony?

I believe a testimony is innate within us, yet, in order to keep it and more fully develop it, Alma taught that we must nourish our testimony with much care.[9] As we do so, "it will get root, and grow up, and bring forth fruit."[10] Without this, "it withers away."[11]

Each beloved member of the First Presidency has provided us with direction on how to keep a testimony.

President Henry B. Eyring lovingly taught us that "feasting on the word of God, heartfelt prayer, and obedience to the Lord's commandments must be applied evenly and continually for your testimony to grow and prosper."[12]

President Dallin H. Oaks reminded us that to retain our testimony, "we need to partake of the sacrament each week (see D&C 59:9) to qualify for the precious promise that we will 'always have his Spirit to be with [us]' (D&C 20:77)."[13]

And President Russell M. Nelson kindly counseled recently:

"Feed [your testimony] truth. . . .

". . . Nourish yourself in the words of ancient and modern prophets. Ask the Lord to teach you how to hear Him better. Spend more time in the temple and in family history work.

". . . Make your testimony your highest priority."[14]

Conclusion

My beloved brothers and sisters, I promise that as you more fully understand what a testimony is, and as you share it, you will overcome obstacles of uncertainty and fear, enabling you to nurture and keep this most precious possession, your testimony.

We are blessed to have countless examples of ancient and modern-day prophets who have boldly borne their testimonies.

Following Christ's death, Peter stood and testified:

"Be it known unto you all . . . that by the name of Jesus Christ of Nazareth, whom ye crucified, whom God raised from the dead, . . . doth this man stand here before you. . . .

". . . For there is none other name under heaven given among men, whereby we must be saved."[15]

Amulek, following Alma's sermon on faith, stated powerfully: "I will testify unto you of myself that these things are true. Behold, I say unto you, that I do know that Christ shall come among the children of men, . . . and that he shall atone for the sins of the world; for the Lord God hath spoken it."[16]

Joseph Smith and Sidney Rigdon, upon witnessing a glorious vision of the resurrected Savior, testified:

"And now, after the many testimonies which have been given of him, this is the testimony, last of all, which we give of him: That he lives!

"For we saw him, even on the right hand of God; and we heard the voice bearing record that he is the Only Begotten of the Father."[17]

Brothers and sisters, I invite you to seek opportunities to bear your testimony in word and in deed. Such an opportunity came to me recently, at the end of a meeting with the mayor of a capital city in South America, in his chambers with a number of his cabinet officials. As we concluded with very cordial feelings, I hesitantly thought I should share my testimony. Following the prompting, I offered a witness that Jesus Christ is the Son of the living God and the Savior of the world. Everything changed at that moment. The Spirit in the room was undeniable. It seemed everyone was touched. "The Comforter . . . beareth record of the Father and of the Son."[18] I am so grateful I summoned the courage to bear my testimony.

When a moment like this comes, grab it and embrace it. You will feel the warmth of the Comforter inside you when you do.

I offer my testimony and witness to you—God is our Heavenly Father, Jesus Christ lives, and The Church of Jesus Christ of Latter-day Saints is God's Church on the earth today led by our dear prophet, President Russell M. Nelson. In the name of Jesus Christ, amen.

Notes

1. See Romans 1:16.
2. Personal conversation and correspondence with Kevin Mumford, Sept. 2022; see also Kevin Mumford, "How I Know: I'm Not Ashamed," *New Era*, Jan. 1999, 26–27.
3. 1 Kings 19:12.
4. Moroni 10:32.
5. See Mosiah 18:9.
6. Matthew Cowley, in Joseph Fielding McConkie, *Here We Stand* (1995), 189.
7. Dallin H. Oaks, "Testimony," *Ensign* or *Liahona*, May 2008, 27.
8. 2 Timothy 1:7–8.

9. See Alma 32:37.
10. Alma 32:37.
11. Alma 32:38.
12. Henry B. Eyring, "A Living Testimony," *Ensign* or *Liahona*, May 2011, 126.
13. Dallin H. Oaks, "Testimony," *Ensign* or *Liahona*, May 2008, 27.
14. Russell M. Nelson, "Choices for Eternity" (worldwide devotional for young adults, May 15, 2022), broadcasts.ChurchofJesusChrist.org.
15. Acts 4:10, 12.
16. Alma 34:8.
17. Doctrine and Covenants 76:22–23.
18. Doctrine and Covenants 42:17.

WE CAN DO HARD THINGS THROUGH HIM

ELDER ISAAC K. MORRISON
Of the Seventy

During the Savior's earthly ministry, He noticed a man who was blind. Jesus's disciples asked, "Master, who did sin, this man, or his parents, that he was born blind?"

The Savior's firm, loving, and sincere answer reassures us that He is mindful of our struggles: "Neither hath this man sinned, nor his parents: but that the works of God should be made manifest in him."[1]

While some challenges may come because of willful disobedience, we know that many of life's challenges come because of other reasons. Whatever the source of our challenges, they can be a golden opportunity to grow.

Our family has not been spared the adversities of life. Growing up, I admired large families. Such families felt appealing to me, especially when I found the Church in my teens through my maternal uncle, Sarfo, and his wife in Takoradi, Ghana.

When Hannah and I were married, we desired the fulfillment of our patriarchal blessings, which indicated that we would be blessed with many children. However, prior to the birth of our third boy, it became medically clear that Hannah would not be able to have another baby. Gratefully, though Kenneth was born in a life-threatening situation to both him and his mother, he arrived safely, and his mother recovered. He was able to begin to fully participate in our family life—including Church attendance, daily family prayers, scripture study, home evening, and wholesome recreational activities.

Though we had to adjust our expectations of a large family, it was a joy to put into practice the teachings from "The Family: A Proclamation to the World" with our three beloved children. Following those teachings added much meaning to my growing faith.

As the proclamation states: "Marriage between man and woman

is essential to His eternal plan. Children are entitled to birth within the bonds of matrimony, and to be reared by a father and a mother who honor marital vows with complete fidelity."[2] As we put these principles into practice, we were blessed.

However, one weekend during my service as a stake president, we experienced perhaps the worst trial parents can face. Our family returned from a Church activity and gathered for lunch. Then our three boys went out within our compound to play.

My wife felt repeated impressions that something might be wrong. She asked me to check on the children while we were washing the dishes. I felt they were safe since we could hear their voices of excitement from their play.

When we both finally went to check on our sons, to our dismay we found little 18-month-old Kenneth helpless in a bucket of water, unseen by his brothers. We rushed him to the hospital, but all attempts to revive him proved futile.

We were devastated that we would not have the opportunity to raise our precious child during this mortal life. Though we knew Kenneth would be part of our family eternally, I found myself questioning why God would let this tragedy happen to me when I was doing all I could to magnify my calling. I had just come home from fulfilling one of my duties in ministering to the Saints. Why couldn't God look upon my service and save our son and our family from this tragedy? The more I thought about it, the more bitter I became.

My wife never blamed me for not responding to her promptings, but I learned a life-changing lesson and made two rules, never to be broken:

Rule 1: Listen to and heed the promptings of your wife.

Rule 2: If you are not sure for any reason, refer to rule number 1.

Though the experience was shattering and we continue to grieve, our overwhelming burden was eventually eased.[3] My wife and I learned specific lessons from our loss. We came to feel united and bound by our temple covenants; we know we can claim Kenneth as ours in the next world because he was born in the covenant. We also gained experience necessary to minister to others and empathize with their pain. I testify that our bitterness has since dispersed as we exercised faith in the Lord. Our experience continues to be hard, but we have learned with the Apostle Paul that we "can do all things through Christ which [strengthens us]" if we focus on Him.[4]

President Russell M. Nelson taught, "When the focus of our lives is on God's plan of salvation . . . and Jesus Christ and His gospel, we can feel joy regardless of what is happening—or not happening—in our lives." He further said, "Joy comes from and because of Him."[5]

We can be of good cheer and be filled with peace in our tough times. The love we feel because of the Savior and His Atonement becomes a powerful resource to us in our trying moments. "All that is unfair [and difficult] about life can be made right through the Atonement of Jesus Christ."[6] He commanded, "In the world ye shall have tribulation: but be of good cheer; I have overcome the world."[7] He can help us endure whatever pain, sickness, and trials we face in mortality.

We find many scriptural stories of great and noble leaders, such as Jeremiah, Job, Joseph Smith, and Nephi, who were not spared from the struggles and challenges of mortality. They were mortals who learned to obey the Lord even in harsh conditions.[8]

During the terrible days in Liberty Jail, Joseph Smith cried out: "O God, where art thou? And where is the pavilion that covereth thy hiding place?"[9] The Lord taught Joseph to "endure it well"[10] and promised that if he did, all these things would give him experience and would be for his good.[11]

Reflecting on my own experiences, I realize I have learned some of my best lessons during the hardest times in my life, times that took me out of my comfort zone. Difficulties I encountered as a youth, while learning about the Church through seminary, as a recent convert, and as a full-time missionary and challenges I faced in my education, in striving to magnify my callings, and in raising a family have prepared me for the future. The more I cheerfully respond to difficult circumstances with faith in the Lord, the more I grow in my discipleship.

The hard things in our lives should come as no surprise once we have entered the strait and narrow path.[12] Jesus Christ learned "obedience by the things which he suffered."[13] As we follow Him, especially in our difficult times, we can grow to become more like Him.

One of the covenants we make with the Lord in the temple is to live the law of sacrifice. Sacrifice has always been part of the gospel of Jesus Christ. It is a reminder of the great atoning sacrifice of Jesus Christ for all who have lived or will live on earth.

I know that the Lord always compensates our righteous desires. Remember the many children I was promised in my patriarchal blessing? That blessing is being fulfilled. My wife and I served with several hundred missionaries, from more than 25 countries, in the Ghana Cape Coast Mission. They are as dear to us as if they were literally our own children.

I testify that we grow in our discipleship when we exercise faith in the Lord during difficult times. As we do so, He will mercifully strengthen us and help us carry our burdens. In the name of Jesus Christ, amen.

Notes

1. John 9:2–3.
2. "The Family: A Proclamation to the World," ChurchofJesusChrist.org.
3. See Mosiah 24:14–15.
4. Philippians 4:13.
5. Russell M. Nelson, "Joy and Spiritual Survival," *Ensign* or *Liahona*, Nov. 2016, 82.
6. *Preach My Gospel: A Guide to Missionary Service* (2019), 52.
7. John 16:33.
8. See Job 27:5.
9. Doctrine and Covenants 121:1.
10. Doctrine and Covenants 121:8.
11. See Doctrine and Covenants 122:7.
12. See 2 Nephi 31:19–21.
13. Hebrews 5:8.

BE TRUE TO GOD AND HIS WORK

ELDER QUENTIN L. COOK
Of the Quorum of the Twelve Apostles

Last October, I was assigned, along with President M. Russell Ballard and Elder Jeffrey R. Holland, to visit the United Kingdom, where all three of us served as young missionaries. We had the privilege of teaching and testifying, as well as reliving early Church history in the British Isles, where my great-great-grandfather Heber C. Kimball and his associates were the first missionaries.[1]

President Russell M. Nelson, teasing us about this assignment, noted that it was unusual to assign three Apostles to visit the area where they had served as missionaries in their youth. He acknowledged that all desire to be assigned to visit their original mission. With a big smile on his face, he succinctly explained the precedent that if there is another set of three Apostles who served in the same mission over 60 years ago, then they also may receive a similar assignment.

In preparation for that assignment, I reread the *Life of Heber C. Kimball*, written by his grandson Orson F. Whitney, who later was called to the apostleship. This volume was given to me by my precious mother when I was almost seven years old. We were preparing to attend the dedication of the This Is the Place Monument on July 24, 1947, by President George Albert Smith.[2] She wanted me to know more about my ancestor Heber C. Kimball.

This book contains a profound statement attributed to President Kimball that has significance for our day. Before sharing the statement, let me provide a little background.

While the Prophet Joseph Smith was incarcerated in Liberty Jail, Apostles Brigham Young and Heber C. Kimball had the responsibility, under terribly adverse circumstances, of overseeing the evacuation of the Saints from Missouri. The evacuation was required in large part because of the extermination order issued by Governor Lilburn W. Boggs.[3]

Almost 30 years later Heber C. Kimball, then in the First Presidency, reflecting on this history with a new generation, taught, "Let me say to you, that many of you will see the time when you will have all the trouble, trial and persecution that you can stand, and plenty of opportunities to show that you are *true to God and His work.*"[4]

Heber continued: "To meet the difficulties that are coming, it will be necessary for you to have a knowledge of the truth of this work for yourselves. The difficulties will be of such a character that the man or woman who does not possess this personal knowledge or witness will fall. If you have not got the testimony, live right and call upon the Lord and cease not [until] you [attain] it. If you do not you will not stand. . . . The time will come when no man nor woman will be able to endure on borrowed light. Each will have to be guided by the light within himself. . . . If you don't have it you will not stand; therefore seek for the testimony of Jesus and cleave to it, that when the trying time comes you may not stumble and fall."[5]

We each need a personal testimony of God's work[6] and the seminal role of Jesus Christ. The 76th section of the Doctrine and Covenants refers to the three degrees of glory and compares the celestial glory to the sun. It then compares the terrestrial kingdom to the moon.[7]

It is interesting that the sun has its own light, but the moon is reflected light or "borrowed light." Speaking of the terrestrial kingdom, verse 79 states, "These are they who are not valiant in the testimony of Jesus." We cannot obtain the celestial kingdom and live with God the Father on borrowed light; we need our own testimony of Jesus Christ and His gospel.

We live in a world where iniquity abounds[8] and hearts turn from God because of the precepts of men.[9] One of the most compelling examples in the scriptures of Heber C. Kimball's concerns about seeking a testimony of God's work and Jesus Christ is set forth in Alma's counsel to his three sons—Helaman, Shiblon, and Corianton.[10] Two of his sons had been *true to God and His work.* But one son had made some bad decisions. To me the greatest significance of Alma's counsel is that he was imparting it as a father for the benefit of his own children.

Alma's first concern, like Heber C. Kimball's, was that each have a testimony of Jesus Christ and *be true to God and His work.*

In Alma's remarkable teaching to his son Helaman, he makes a profound promise that those who "put their trust in God shall be supported in their trials, and their troubles, and their afflictions, and shall be lifted up at the last day."[11]

While Alma had received a manifestation where he saw an angel, this is rare. Impressions made by the Holy Ghost are more typical. These impressions can be equally as important as angelic manifestations. President Joseph Fielding Smith taught: "Impressions on the soul that come from the Holy Ghost are far more significant than a vision. When Spirit speaks to spirit, the imprint upon the soul is far more difficult to erase."[12]

This leads us to Alma's counsel to his second son, Shiblon. Shiblon was righteous, like his brother Helaman. The counsel I want to emphasize is Alma 38:12, which reads in part, "See that ye bridle all your passions, that ye may be filled with love."

Bridle is an interesting word. When we ride a horse, we use the bridle to guide it. A good synonym might be to direct, control, or restrain. The Old Testament tells us we shouted for joy when we learned we would have physical bodies.[13] The body is not evil—it is beautiful and essential—but some passions, if not used properly and appropriately bridled, can separate us from *God and His work* and adversely impact our testimony.

Let's talk about two passions in particular—first, anger, and second, lust.[14] It is interesting that both left unbridled or uncontrolled can cause great heartache, diminish the influence of the Spirit, and separate us from God and His work. The adversary takes every opportunity to fill our lives with images of violence and immorality.

In some families, it is not uncommon for an angry husband or wife to hit a spouse or a child. In July, I participated in a United Kingdom All-Party Parliamentary forum in London.[15] Violence against women and youth was highlighted as a significant worldwide problem. In addition to violence, others have engaged in verbal abuse. The proclamation on the family tells us those "who abuse spouse or offspring . . . will one day stand accountable before God."[16]

President Nelson strongly emphasized this yesterday morning.[17]

Please make up your mind that regardless of whether your parents did or did not abuse you, you will not physically or verbally or emotionally abuse your spouse or children.

In our day one of the most significant challenges is contention and verbal abuse related to societal issues. In many cases anger and abusive language have replaced reason, discussion, and civility. Many have abandoned the admonition of the Savior's senior Apostle, Peter, to seek Christlike qualities such as temperance, patience, godliness, brotherly kindness, and charity.[18] They have also abandoned the Christlike quality of humility.

In addition to controlling anger and bridling other passions, we need to lead pure moral lives by controlling our thoughts, language, and actions. We need to avoid pornography, evaluate the appropriateness of what we are streaming in our homes, and avoid every form of sinful conduct.

This brings us to Alma's counsel to his son Corianton. Unlike his brothers, Helaman and Shiblon, Corianton engaged in moral transgression.

Because Corianton had engaged in immorality, it was necessary for Alma to teach him about repentance. He had to teach him the seriousness of sin and then how to repent.[19]

So Alma's preventive counsel was to bridle passions, but his counsel for those who have transgressed was to repent. President Nelson gave members profound counsel on repentance at the April 2019 general conference. He made it clear that daily repentance is integral to our lives. "Repentance is not an event; it is a process. It is the key to happiness and peace of mind," he taught. "Daily repentance is the pathway to purity, and purity brings power."[20] If Corianton had done what President Nelson counseled, he would have repented as soon as he had begun to entertain impure thoughts. Major transgressions would not have occurred.

The concluding counsel that Alma gave to his sons is some of the most important doctrine in all the scriptures. It relates to the Atonement wrought by Jesus Christ.

Alma testified that Christ would take away sin.[21] Without the

Savior's Atonement, the eternal principle of justice would require punishment.[22] Because of the Savior's Atonement, mercy can prevail for those who have repented, and it can allow them to return to the presence of God. We would do well to ponder this wonderful doctrine.

None can return to God by his or her own good works alone; we all need the benefit of the Savior's sacrifice. All have sinned, and it is only through the Atonement of Jesus Christ that we can obtain mercy and live with God.[23]

Alma also gave wonderful counsel to Corianton for all of us who have gone through or will go through the repentance process, regardless of whether the sins are small or as severe as those committed by Corianton. Verse 29 of Alma 42 reads, "And now, my son, I desire that ye should let these things trouble you no more, and only let your sins trouble you, with that trouble which shall bring you down unto repentance."

Corianton heeded Alma's counsel and both repented and served honorably. Because of the Savior's Atonement, healing is available to all.

In Alma's day, in Heber's day, and certainly in our day, we all need to seek our own testimony of Jesus Christ, bridle our passions, repent of our sins, and find peace through the Atonement of Jesus Christ and be true to God and His work.

In a recent talk and again this morning, President Russell M. Nelson said it this way: "I plead with you to take charge of your testimony of Jesus Christ. Work for it. Own it. Care for it. Nurture it so that it will grow. Then watch for miracles to happen in your life."[24]

I am grateful that we will now hear from President Nelson. I testify that President Nelson is the Lord's prophet for our day. I love and treasure the marvelous inspiration and guidance we receive through him.

As an Apostle of the Lord Jesus Christ, I bear my sure witness of the Savior's divinity and the reality of His Atonement in the name of Jesus Christ, amen.

Notes

1. See Ronald K. Esplin, "A Great Work Done in That Land," *Ensign*, July 1987, 20: "On June 13, Elder Kimball, Orson Hyde, Joseph Fielding, and Heber's friend Willard Richards left Kirtland for England. In New York, on June 22, Canadians Isaac Russell, John Goodson, and John Snyder joined them. The seven missionaries then booked passage for Liverpool on the *Garrick*." (See Heber C. Kimball papers, 1837–1866; Willard Richards journals and papers, 1821–1854, Church History Library, Salt Lake City.)
2. The This Is the Place Monument, located on the east side of Salt Lake City, Utah, at the mouth of Emigration Canyon, commemorates the 100th anniversary of the arrival of the Saints into the Salt Lake Valley on July 24, 1847. The monument features statues of Brigham Young, Heber C. Kimball, and Wilford Woodruff.
3. Between 8,000 and 10,000 Latter-day Saints fled Missouri in early 1839 to escape violent acts of vigilantes and mobs. Under the direction of Brigham Young and Heber C. Kimball, a committee was formed to collect supplies, assess needs, and establish routes for the grueling 200-mile (320-km) winter exodus to Illinois. Compassionate residents of the town of Quincy provided temporary refuge for the suffering Saints by way of shelter and food. (See *Saints: The Story of the Church of Jesus Christ in the Latter Days*, vol. 1, *The Standard of Truth, 1815–1846* [2018], 375–77; William G. Hartley, "The Saints' Forced Exodus from Missouri," in Richard Neitzel Holzapfel and Kent P. Jackson, eds., *Joseph Smith: The Prophet and Seer* [2010], 347–89.)
4. In Orson F. Whitney, *Life of Heber C. Kimball: An Apostle, the Father and Founder of the British Mission* (1945), 449; emphasis added.
5. In Orson F. Whitney, *Life of Heber C. Kimball*, 450.
6. See Moses 1:39; see also "The Work of Salvation and Exaltation," section 1.2 in *General Handbook: Serving in The Church of Jesus Christ of Latter-day Saints*, ChurchofJesusChrist.org. We come unto Christ and assist in God's work by living the gospel of Jesus Christ, caring for those in need, inviting all to receive the gospel, and uniting families for eternity. See also Doctrine and Covenants 110, which sets forth the keys that were given for the work of salvation.
7. See also 1 Corinthians 15:40–41.
8. See Doctrine and Covenants 45:27.
9. See Doctrine and Covenants 45:29.
10. Alma was the son of Alma the prophet. He was the chief judge of the nation and high priest and prophet. He experienced a miraculous conversion as a young man.
11. Alma 36:3.
12. Joseph Fielding Smith, "The First Presidency and the Council of the Twelve," *Improvement Era*, Nov. 1966, 979.
13. See Job 38:7.
14. See Alma 39:9. Alma instructs Corianton, "Go no more after the [lust] of your eyes."
15. All-Party Parliamentary Group, Parliamentary sessions, Tuesday, July 5, 2022, "Preventing Violence and Promoting Freedom of Belief."
16. "The Family: A Proclamation to the World," ChurchofJesusChrist.org; see also Patrick Kearon, "He Is Risen with Healing in His Wings: We Can Be More Than Conquerors," *Liahona*, May 2022, 37–39.
17. See Russell M. Nelson, "What Is True?," *Liahona*, Nov. 2022, 29.
18. See 2 Peter 1:5–10.
19. See Alma 39:9.
20. Russell M. Nelson, "We Can Do Better and Be Better," *Ensign* or *Liahona*, May 2019, 67, 68.
21. See Alma 39:15.
22. See Alma 42:16.
23. See 2 Nephi 25:23.
24. Russell M. Nelson, Facebook, Aug. 1, 2022, facebook.com/russell.m.nelson; Twitter, Aug. 1, 2022, twitter.com/nelsonrussellm; Instagram, Aug. 1, 2022, instagram.com/russellmnelson; see also "Choices for Eternity" (worldwide devotional for young adults, May 15, 2022), broadcasts.ChurchofJesusChrist.org.

FOCUS ON THE TEMPLE

PRESIDENT RUSSELL M. NELSON

President of The Church of Jesus Christ of Latter-day Saints

Dear brothers and sisters, during these five magnificent sessions of general conference, we have once again experienced that the heavens are open! I pray that you have recorded your impressions and will follow through with them. Our Heavenly Father and His Beloved Son, Jesus Christ, stand ready to help you. I urge you to increase your efforts to seek Their help.

Recently, Sister Nelson and I had the opportunity to preview the new season 4 of the *Book of Mormon Videos* series.[1] We were inspired by them! May I show you a brief excerpt from the scene depicting the Savior's appearance to the Nephites.

It is significant that the Savior chose to appear to the people at the temple. It is His house. It is filled with His power. Let us never lose sight of what the Lord is doing for us now. He is making His temples more accessible. He is accelerating the pace at which we are building temples. He is increasing our ability to help gather Israel. He is also making it easier for each of us to become spiritually refined. I promise that increased time in the temple will bless your life in ways nothing else can.

We currently have 168 operating temples and 53 new temples under construction and another 54 in the preconstruction design phase![2] I am pleased to announce our plans to build a new temple in each of the following locations: Busan, Korea; Naga, Philippines; Santiago, Philippines; Eket, Nigeria; Chiclayo, Peru; Buenos Aires City Center, Argentina; Londrina, Brazil; Ribeirão Prêto, Brazil; Huehuetenango, Guatemala; Jacksonville, Florida; Grand Rapids, Michigan; Prosper, Texas; Lone Mountain, Nevada; and Tacoma, Washington.

We are also planning to build multiple temples in selected large metropolitan areas where travel time to an existing temple is a major challenge. Therefore, I am pleased to announce four additional locations near Mexico City where new temples will be built in Cuernavaca, Pachuca, Toluca, and Tula.

My dear brothers and sisters, may you focus on the temple in ways you never have before. I bless you to grow closer to God and Jesus Christ every day. I love you. May God be with you until we meet again, I pray in the sacred name of Jesus Christ, amen.

Notes

1. These new videos will be available in many languages on Gospel Library and other channels. Episodes will be published on a weekly basis after conference.
2. As of October 1, 2022, four more temples are being renovated (St. George Utah, Manti Utah, Salt Lake, and Columbus Ohio), and three are awaiting dedication (Hamilton New Zealand, Quito Ecuador, and Belém Brazil).

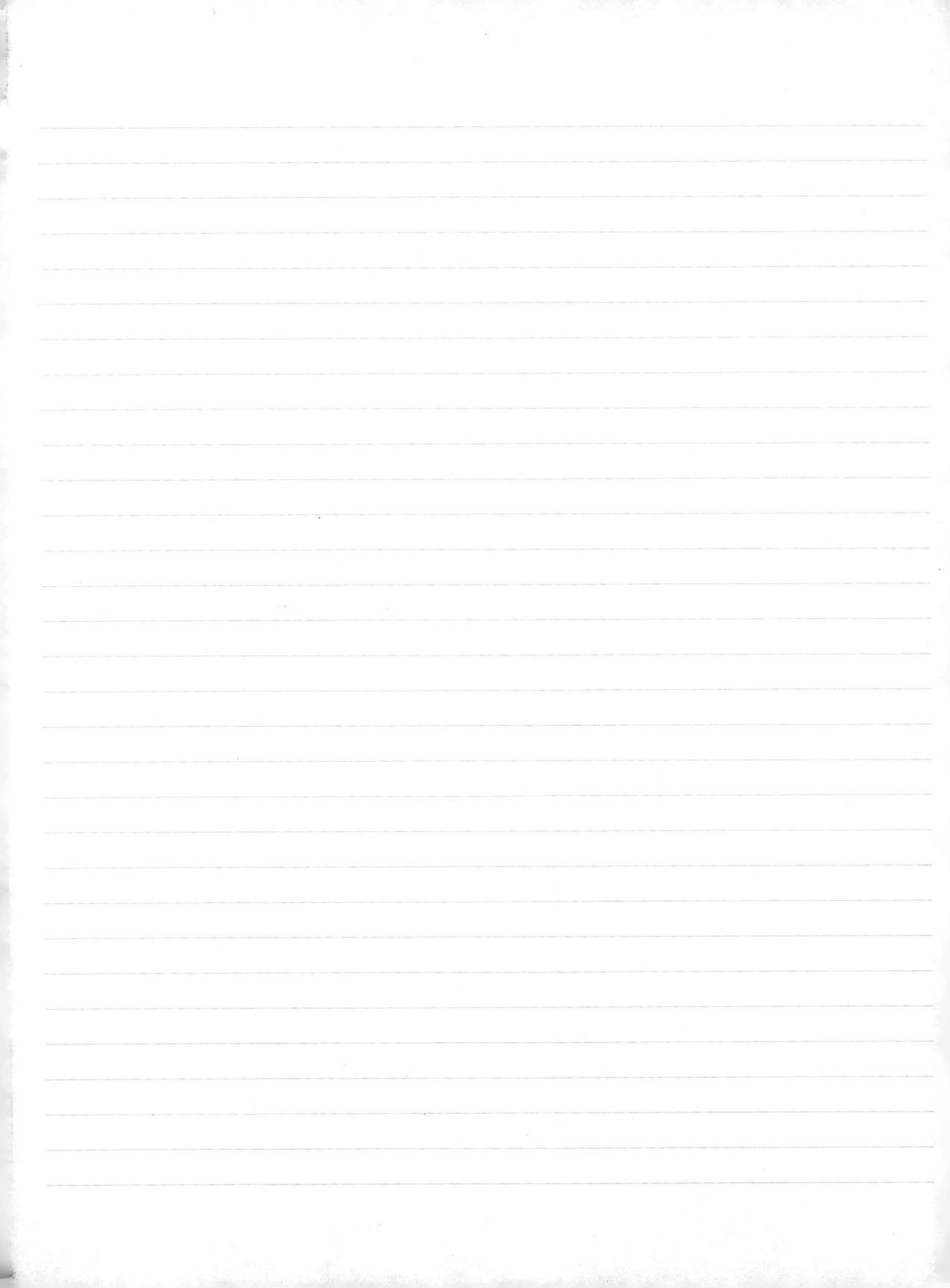